SO-AUX-909

ROCK'n'IR OLL
LOVE STORIES

ROCK 'n' ROLL LOVE STORIES

TRUE TALES OF THE PASSION AND DRAMA BEHIND THE STAGE ACTS

GILL PAUL

PROSPERO BOOKS

For Daisy Bata, the coolest of the cool

Published by Prospero Books,
by arrangement with

Ivy Press

All rights reserved. No part of this publication may be reproduced,
stored in a retrieval system, or transmitted, in any form or by any
means, electronic, mechanical, photocopying, recording, or otherwise,
without prior written permission from the publisher.

© 2014 by Ivy Press Limited

This book was conceived, designed, and produced by
Ivy Press
210 High Street, Lewes,
East Sussex BN7 2NS, U.K.
www.ivypress.co.uk

Creative Director Peter Bridgewater

Publisher Susan Kelly

Art Director Wayne Blades

Senior Editor Jayne Ansell

Designer Andrew Milne

Picture Researcher Katie Greenwood

ISBN 978-1-55-267-625-7

Prospero Books
468 King Street West, Suite 500
Toronto, Ontario M5V 1L8
Canada

Manufactured in China
Color origination by Ivy Press Reprographics

10 9 8 7 6 5 4 3 2 1

CONTENTS

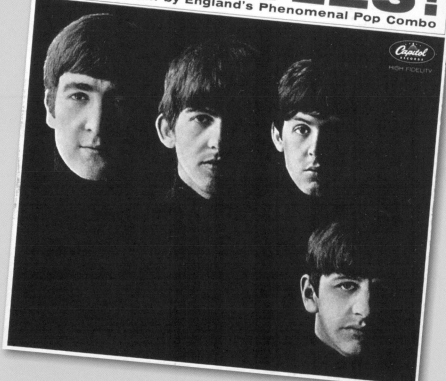

INTRODUCTION

Just about every rock song is about love—loss of it, the need for it, and how great it is when you find it—but rock stars don't seem on the whole to be great lovers. The pressures of long world tours, the ready availability of sexually willing groupies, and spending more time with the band than the family all place a strain that only the strongest relationships can survive. On top of that, drugs and booze are traditionally part and parcel of the rock-star lifestyle, and both invariably make the user self-centered and antisocial, which is hardly conducive to romance and passion. Add to the mix the tendency for some styles of rock music to express a negativity and a cynicism about traditional monogamy. Boy meets girl, they fall in love and get married for life? That is too square and boring. Yet finding love that lasts is one of life's greatest urges. How can rock stars achieve this without damaging their cool credentials?

The roots of rock

Rock 'n' roll (a term with sexual origins) exploded into the mainstream via a mix of Bill Haley's "Rock Around the Clock" (its lyrics basically telling you to have sex all night) and Elvis gyrating his pelvis. It was born out of the black delta blues of the American South and emerged in the early 1950s when black and white folk began listening to each other's music (often without realizing it) on radio stations that started playing a mixture of styles, from rhythm and blues to swing, gospel, country, and folk. Music historians argue about the first rock 'n' roll record— was it "Rocket 88" (1951) by Ike Turner and his Kings of Rhythm? Or was it Roy Brown's "Good Rockin' Tonight" (1947) or Bill Haley's "Crazy Man, Crazy" (1953)? It depends how you define it, but the key musical difference was the use of a guitar as the lead instrument and a blues rhythm with an accentuated backbeat, usually from a snare drum. It took a few years

OPPOSITE
Bill Haley. Conspiracy theorists believed rock 'n' roll was part of a communist plot to corrupt American youth, and the FBI tried to dig up dirt on him.

BELOW
Chuck Berry's debut album, which came out in May 1957, included the hit "School Day (Ring! Ring! Goes the Bell)." Fifteen years later, he released the song "My Ding-a-Ling" with notorious double entendre lyrics.

Rock 'n' roll dancing developed from a combination of the Lindy Hop, jive, swing, and boogie-woogie. Throwing your partner around (for the guy) and decent underwear (for the girl) were de rigueur.

to catch on, but when it did the sound went stratospheric with hits by Elvis, Little Richard, Jerry Lee Lewis, Chuck Berry, and dozens of others giving youngsters fast dance rhythms via the new medium of television. *American Bandstand,* which first aired in 1952, showed teenagers rocking to the latest top 40 hits, and gave bands the ideal platform to promote their records.

It certainly helped that the authorities were disapproving, even downright scandalized. Elvis's suggestive hip movements were seen as so provocative that he was only shown from the waist up on television, and he was strenuously criticized by religious groups across the nation. Frank Sinatra firmly identified himself as one of the older generation by condemning the new music. "It is sung, played, and written for the most part by cretinous goons," he said, criticizing the "sly, lewd, in plain fact, dirty lyrics" and calling it "the most brutal, ugly, desperate, vicious form of expression it has ever been my misfortune to hear." Boy, was he out of step with the times!

Jerry Lee Lewis, aged twenty-two, with Myra, his thirteen-year-old cousin and third wife. She was married to him for thirteen years and bore him two children. After they divorced, he married four more times.

Teenagers of the postwar generation rejected their parents' wartime values of duty and austerity. They were now growing up in relatively affluent circumstances and had money in their pockets to buy the latest vinyl records, especially the 45rpm singles that were first introduced in 1949. They fell out with their parents, whom they felt didn't understand them, and abandoned religion in their droves. Rock 'n' roll stars wrote songs for this generation of rebels without a cause, daring to say that school was boring and oppressive, parents were uncool dinosaurs, and that sex in the back seat of a car was a whole lot of fun. Their influence gradually extended into lots of other areas beyond music: initially fashion and language, then civil rights, attitudes to war and politics, feminism, and sexual freedom. There were a few scandals that gave the record companies problems, and the bosses began to search for good-looking, squeaky-clean performers who wouldn't upset anyone—like

WILD MEN OF ROCK 'N' ROLL

Known for his lively performances in which he pounded the piano keys and kicked the piano stool away, Jerry Lee Lewis pushed the outrageous act too far when he took his thirteen-year-old cousin Myra as his third wife. The record company wanted to hush it up, but he announced it to the press during a tour of Britain. Although he lied and said that Myra was fifteen, that was still underage and the furor was enough to bring his career to a halt from which it never really regained momentum. Little Richard wore brightly colored suits, high-heeled shoes, and a pompadour hairstyle for his wild stage act, but his sexual predilections saw him charged with lewd conduct for voyeurism and masturbating in public before he found God and became a reformed character. Screamin' Jay Hawkins used to jump out of coffins to the accompaniment of flashes and bangs, throwing wriggling things he claimed were worms into the audience. He married countless times, never bothering to divorce the women in question before moving on. After his death, a record seventy-five children came forward to claim a part of his estate.

ABOVE
*Jimi Hendrix loved his
guitars so much that
he often took one to
bed with him. He was
famous for his onstage
tricks, such as playing
with his teeth or while
holding the guitar
behind his back.*

Bobby Vee, Frankie Avalon,
and, in the UK, Cliff Richard.
But the teenagers knew what
they wanted, and for lots of
them it was rebellion—and sex.

The Sexual Revolution

Attitudes to sex were changing
fast in the 1960s, not least after
the first birth-control pills were
prescribed in 1960, giving
women a way of preventing
unwanted pregnancy, and toward
the end of the decade abortion
was legalized in many countries.
Seizing the moment, in 1953
Hugh Hefner had begun to
popularize pornography by
founding *Playboy* magazine,
and he later opened clubs in
which men were served by
Playboy bunnies with fluffy
tails (Debbie Harry worked
as one for a while). Couples
began marrying later in life,
which left a large population
of kids in their late teens and early twenties who were happily
unmarried and sexually aware. And rock songs urged them to
have sex: "(Come on baby) light my fire" sang Jim Morrison,
while The Rolling Stones urged, "Let's Spend the Night
Together," and Bob Dylan crooned "Lay, Lady, Lay." On stage,
the hit show of 1967 was the musical *Hair*, which was liberally
sprinkled with nudity, profanity, and much smoking of weed.
The message to young people was loud and clear—if you're
not having sex, you're missing out.

The music world is seen as glamorous and musicians have
always attracted attention from the opposite sex, but teenage
girls began to react to the sexualized rock 'n' roll acts with
hysteria. It wasn't an entirely new phenomenon: composer
Franz Liszt in the 1840s and Frank Sinatra a century later had

inspired frenzied reactions from fans, but the girls who screamed at Elvis concerts were younger and were giving vent to a repressed sexuality for which they had no other release. Beatles fans took this adulation to new levels of hysteria, with some girls fainting and needing medical attention at their concerts— the term Beatlemania was nothing less than accurate. Meanwhile, the fans who could find their way backstage were getting a whole new level of attention from their heroes. Bill Wyman of The Rolling Stones first coined the term "groupie" in 1965 during the band's tour of Australia. In an era when good girls tried to keep it quiet if they were doing "it" so as not to get a bad name, groupies often boasted of their conquests. Devon Wilson, Pamela Des Barres, and Bebe Buell were famous '60s and '70s groupies who targeted a list that included Jimi Hendrix, Mick Jagger, Eric Clapton, Jim Morrison, Jimmy Page of Led Zeppelin, and Keith Moon of The Who—and the stars were more than willing to oblige. In the late '60s era of "free love," and with opportunity being thrust upon them, few rock stars stayed faithful to their wife or girlfriend. There was an unspoken pact: "What happens on tour, stays on tour." Even if the girlfriends found out about infidelities, as Marianne Faithfull explained, it was considered "unhip and middle class" to complain.

BELOW
Beatlemania hits Toronto, September 1964, on the band's first North American tour. Newspapers rolled out psychologists to talk about the girls' repressed sexuality and speculate on whether they had orgasms while watching their idols.

So far the Sexual Revolution wasn't entirely working in women's favor, because the old double standard prevailed. While boys could be seen as charming lotharios, Faithfull was vilified in the press after she was found naked and wrapped in a fur rug when police raided Keith Richards's house, and Carly Simon attracted sexist headlines when she dared to have serial relationships with a few rock stars. The music industry was male-dominated and women had to work twice as hard as their male counterparts to reach the top. It was all right for men to write sexually suggestive lyrics but radio stations refused to play Carole King's "I Feel the Earth Move" and "(You Make Me Feel Like) A Natural Woman." It would be the 1980s before a female star like Madonna would be allowed to flaunt her sexuality on stage just as blatantly as men had back in the '60s.

> ## "FIFTEEN MINUTES AFTER TAKING A FEW PILLS THE WHOLE WORLD TOOK ON A ROSY GLOW..."
> HANK WILLIAMS, JR.

Sweet Mary Jane

Rock stars work antisocial hours and are under pressure to perform on tours that are booked months in advance. With hundreds or thousands of tickets sold for a gig, they can't cancel because they feel tired or unwell, so back in the '50s and '60s, an amphetamine shot or a prescription for some uppers from a sympathetic doctor would be just perfect. Valium hit the market in 1960 and soon became the most prescribed drug of all time; this and other sedatives were useful for musicians who needed to come down and get some sleep after a show. Addictive prescription drugs weren't the sole preserve of musicians, of course, with John F. Kennedy among those who regulated their energy levels with drugs supplied by medics. Hank Williams, Jr. explained the appeal: "Fifteen minutes after taking a few pills the whole world took on a rosy glow ... With liquor you'd always have to face the inevitable morning after ... With pills you can postpone that morning after for a hell of a long time, weeks in fact, and also you could play the shows all night if you wanted to." The fact that they were addictive and caused long-term damage to health took a while to be recognized, but in the meantime, rock stars' girlfriends and wives were faced with partners who were either

OPPOSITE
Jim Morrison never married but had a long-term partner called Pamela Courson, who found him dead in the bathtub in their Paris apartment in 1971. There was no autopsy, but she claimed he died after accidentally inhaling some heroin, mistaking it for cocaine.

15

ABOVE
Janis Joplin died in October 1970, just sixteen days after Jimi Hendrix, after overdosing on an extra-potent batch of heroin. Her raw, powerful stage performances inspired dozens of female musicians who came after her.

the life and soul of the party or sleepwalking zombies, depending on which pills they had popped.

During the '50s and early '60s, the CIA had been experimenting with the mind-altering properties of LSD, and it was only a matter of time before this powerful hallucinogen, popularly known as acid, leaked into the illegal drugs market on the nation's streets. At the same time marijuana was becoming more widely available, with the prime users being white middle-class college kids. Smoking weed and taking LSD spread in the US first of all, then made their way across the Atlantic. Pattie Boyd claims that Bob Dylan introduced The Beatles to the joys of marijuana, while it was their dentist who first gave her and George Harrison some tabs of acid to try. Songs like The Beatles' "Got to Get You Into My Life" (described by Paul McCartney as "an ode to pot"), Bob Dylan's "Rainy Day Women #12 & 35," and Jimi Hendrix's "Purple Haze," among others, normalized drug use and gave it social acceptance. Timothy Leary called on 30,000 hippies to "Turn on, tune in, drop out" in San Francisco in 1967, and everyone knows the saying that if you can remember the '60s, you weren't really there.

By the end of the decade, heroin had started flooding the US drugs market, brought in by crime families from the south of Italy and France, and it was soon cheap and plentiful on the streets of New York. James Taylor and Lou Reed were among the musicians who started experimenting with the drug and then struggled to break free of its grip. Everyone could see the damage being done but stoned rock stars, stick thin and with huge shadows under their eyes, still had a kind of rock 'n' roll kudos—even after the first ones started dying of their addictions. Hendrix, Morrison, Janis Joplin, Billy Murcia of the New York Dolls, Sid Vicious—the list of casualties grew longer as the '70s progressed. Record companies and individual artists'

OPPOSITE
Another rock 'n' roll casualty—Ian Curtis of Joy Division hanged himself in May 1980, just before the band were due to depart for their first American tour. He was found by his wife, Deborah.

managers tried to pressure their stars to go into rehab, concerned about losing their investment. Meanwhile, heroin addiction didn't do a lot for rock stars' relationships. Either one partner was forever pleading with the other to get "clean" or they were both users, sharing needles and pooling their dealer contacts—no matter which way it worked, the heroin took priority.

Keeping it real

During the late '60s, hippies hoped to use music to fight racism, protest against war, and try to build a new society in which love and freedom of speech were more important than money and power. Bob Dylan's "The Times They Are a-Changin'" summed up the mood, and Woodstock was the moment when it seemed to come together. Heavy metal bands of the '70s chose dark and depressing themes for their lyrics, sometimes combined with

STORIES BEHIND LOVE SONGS

Songwriter Doc Pomus, who was crippled by polio, wrote "Save the Last Dance for Me" (recorded by The Drifters) about watching his wife dance with other men, a song in which he reminds her that they will still be going home together. Eric Clapton wrote "Wonderful Tonight" while waiting for Pattie Boyd as she tried to decide what to wear for an evening out. Bob Dylan wrote "Don't Think Twice, It's Alright" when he was missing his girlfriend Suze Rotolo, who had just extended her stay in Italy. Ian Curtis of Joy Division wrote the poignant song "Love Will Tear Us Apart" about his difficult relationship with his wife Deborah, and after his suicide she had the title carved on his tombstone. On a less romantic note, Bob Marley's girlfriend claimed "I Shot the Sheriff" was about her fights with the singer over birth control, with Sheriff the name of the doctor who wouldn't let Bob "plant his seed." Sting wrote "Every Breath You Take" about an obsessive, unhealthy relationship and was astonished when he heard it had become a favorite track for couples to slow-dance to at their weddings.

ROCK STARS FEELING LIKE SERFS

During the '60s and '70s, many artists found they had signed record contracts that made them employees of the record companies, producing "work for hire" in return for a salary and expenses. This meant the company owned the copyright on the songs, rather than the artist; the company had creative control over the artist's output, and received the profits not just from records but also from tours and merchandising. The companies argued they had taken the risk in bankrolling a new artist and deserved to reap the rewards, but a number of high-profile court cases hit the headlines. David Bowie sold over a million copies of *Ziggy Stardust* but had to live on "loose change," and when he left his record company in 1975 after a legal dispute that lasted several months, he was forced to surrender millions of dollars of his future earnings. Lyle Lovett claimed to have sold 4.6 million records without seeing a cent, and he was not alone. Many musicians were being driven around in limos and staying in hotels, but didn't have two pennies to rub together. Willie Nelson, Marvin Gaye, Meat Loaf, Toni Braxton, and Billy Joel are among the many rock stars who have been driven to declare bankruptcy, for whatever reason.

Wagneresque folkloric symbolism, and accompanied them with a loud, distorted guitar sound and a howling theatrical lead singer (who might even bite off a bat's head on stage, as Black Sabbath's Ozzy Osborne once did). At around the same time, glam rock brought camp, glittery clothing and a reassessment of gender roles, reaching out to teenagers who might be questioning their sexuality. And in the second half of the '70s, punk expressed a hatred for society; there was no future for young people so what was the point of anything? The '80s brought MTV and a focus on surface appearance and slick dance moves, but teenage angst and despair once again found a voice in the '90s with grunge. If there is any message that unites all forms of rock music, it is telling teenagers, "Your parents are boring, and you are cool." And for that, rock stars have to maintain an authenticity in fans' eyes and not sell out their principles.

Fans could learn about the lifestyles and opinions of their favorite stars through magazines such as *Rolling Stone* (founded in 1967), *Spin* (1982–2012), and, in the UK, *New Musical Express* (from March 1952). Whereas movie stars had been trendsetters in the past, suddenly musicians were stepping into the role, and the public were fascinated by their homes, clothes, hairstyles, the cars they drove, and their relationships. Did they correspond with the onstage persona and the sentiments in the lyrics? It was yet one more pressure on rock-star relationships when the image had to carry through into their private lives. And being in the public eye is tough anyway, especially if you first hear about your partner's infidelities when a journalist calls you for a quote about them.

So the odds are stacked against rock stars in love—and yet some of them manage to make it work. Charlie Watts, drummer with The Rolling Stones, married Shirley in 1964 and has reportedly been faithful ever since, in spite of the notorious serial womanizing of some of the other members of the band. Ozzy and Sharon Osborne have been married since 1982, with Sharon nursing and cajoling the singer through his drug and alcohol addictions. Jon Bon Jovi has been married to his childhood sweetheart since 1989, and Bono met his wife, Alison Hewson, at high school and married her in 1982. David Bowie, Keith Richards, Neil Young, Alice Cooper, Michael Anthony, Sting, and Ringo Starr have all made it past their twentieth wedding anniversaries without calling in the divorce lawyers, but most are not so lucky in love—although at least when it all falls apart, they have plenty of material for the next hit song.

ABOVE
Bob Guccione, Jr. with the first edition of Spin, May 1985. The magazine helped to promote many new artists.

BELOW
David and Angie Bowie. Their marriage lasted throughout the '70s although both claimed to be bisexual.

JOHNNY CASH
&
JUNE CARTER

ROCK 'N' ROLL

J.R. CASH

Born: February 26, 1932
Kingsland, Arkansas

Died: September 12, 2003
Nashville, Tennessee

VALERIE JUNE CARTER

Born: June 23, 1929
Maces Spring, Virginia

Died: May 15, 2003
Nashville, Tennessee

Married: March 1, 1968
Franklin, Kentucky

HE'D PUT JUNE THROUGH A LOT OVER THE YEARS
BUT SHE NEVER TURNED HER BACK ON HIM

**June told Johnny categorically that she would only marry him
if he cleaned up his act, weaning himself off the handfuls of uppers
and downers that kept him going. But his reliance on them was
such that it was easier said than done.**

Johnny's childhood was scarred down the middle
by an appalling tragedy that occurred when he
was twelve years old. The family were hardworking
farmers with a smallholding in Dyess, Arkansas, and
Johnny was the fourth of seven children, christened
with the initials J.R. rather than a name, which was not
unusual for the area. He was closest to Jack, who was
three years older than him, later writing in his
autobiography, "I suppose no two boys in a family
were ever closer to one another or loved each other
more than me and my brother Jack." On May 12,
1944, Johnny decided to go fishing and urged Jack to
come with him, but Jack had agreed to go to the high-school
agriculture workshop to cut logs as fence posts, a job that
would earn him $3 to contribute to the ever-tight family
budget. During the day, as Jack worked unsupervised, he was
somehow yanked onto the huge spinning circular saw and it
sliced right into his abdomen. He was rushed to hospital but
the injuries were so severe doctors could only sew him up and
ease the pain with morphine. He lasted a week before dying
of blood poisoning, and in his final hours he talked of seeing
visions of a beautiful city and hearing angels singing. The
tragedy burned itself into Johnny's brain and informed his
religious beliefs as well as giving his character a dark side,
a sadness that could never be entirely assuaged.

The family was musical, and Johnny grew up listening to his
mother singing hymns and popular songs. His eldest brother
Roy was in a band, but although he loved music Johnny
decided he wanted a stable job with regular pay and after
leaving school he enlisted in the US Air Force. While training
in Texas he met a girl called Vivian Liberto at a roller-skating
rink and they dated for just two weeks before he was posted
overseas to Germany. The romance continued over the next
three years via hundreds of letters, in one of which Johnny

ABOVE
*June's religious faith
was one of the most
important things in her
life. Johnny called her
a "prayer warrior."*

OPPOSITE
*Johnny, the Man in
Black, was either the life
and soul of the party or
he was depressed and
self-destructive—there
was no middle way.*

ABOVE
*Johnny with his wife
Vivian and daughters
Rosanne and Kathy
in 1957. Vivian was
a homemaker who
didn't like him going
away on tour.*

proposed. Finally, he returned to the US and on August 7, 1954, they were married in a Catholic ceremony presided over by Vivian's uncle, who was a priest. They settled in Memphis, Tennessee, where Johnny took a job selling electrical appliances door to door. But in Germany he had played in a band called the Landsberg Barbarians and he'd caught the music bug. On returning home he decided to try to break into the music industry, along with two friends with whom he had formed a band. Sam Phillips of a small but influential label called Sun Records released their first single, "Hey, Porter," in June 1955, just a month after the birth of Johnny and Vivian's first child, a daughter called Rosanne. He followed it up with two of his best songs, "Folsom Prison Blues" and "I Walk the Line," which raced up the country charts and crossed over into the pop charts as well. Johnny was on his way to the top.

"I Walk the Line" was such a success that in 1956 Johnny was invited to appear in the prestigious Grand Ole Opry, a weekly concert staged in Nashville, Tennessee featuring all the big names in country music. It was backstage at the Grand Ole Opry that he met June Carter, a member of the family group Mother Maybelle and the Carter Sisters. She was immediately taken with this tall, distinctive-looking man wearing a simple black jacket and pants without any of the sequins some country music stars favored. She liked the way he chatted to the crowd between numbers, and she loved his deep, soulful voice. He was obviously impressed with her, too, because he told her that evening they would be married one day—an odd comment given that they were both devout Christians who believed marriage should be for life.

The Man in Black

Music was in June Carter's blood. Her mother, Maybelle, was a member of The Carter Family, a traditional folk group who achieved great acclaim in the late 1920s and 1930s playing at local radio stations and concert halls. When she was ten years old June joined them, along with her sisters Helen and Anita, who were still so tiny they had to stand on boxes to reach the microphones. The group broke up in 1944, but Maybelle and her daughters continued to perform under the title Mother Maybelle and the Carter Sisters, and her brother Doc and cousin Carl joined them in 1945. June was bright and bubbly, with a natural talent for comedy. She often made radio announcements and recorded commercials as well as singing. Hers wasn't the strongest singing voice in the group but she was the funniest character, entertaining the crowd between numbers with a comic routine or impression. They often appeared at the Grand Ole Opry and toured with up-and-coming singer Elvis Presley despite his musical style being quite different from their normal country fare.

THE GRAND OLE OPRY

Nashville's Grand Ole Opry is a live event that regularly sells out, featuring country music, folk, and gospel as well as comedy skits; it is also broadcast on the world's longest-running radio show. Beginning in 1925 as a barn dance, it has changed venue several times over the decades, but continues to draw new generations of musicians to the present day. In the early years, regular bands included the Fruit Jar Drinkers with their red-hot fiddle playing, and the Possum Hunters with Dr. Humphrey Bate (the first-ever Grand Ole Opry performer). In October 1954, Elvis Presley appeared there but his brand of "rockabilly" music and suggestive hip gyrations didn't go down too well with the crowd and the manager suggested he went back to driving trucks.

Being made a member of the Grand Ole Opry is the pinnacle of achievement for a country star, and Johnny and June were among those so honored. Johnny was banned after an incident in 1965 in which he smashed the lights with his microphone, but was later allowed to perform again.

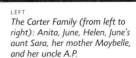

LEFT
The Carter Family (from left to right): Anita, June, Helen, June's aunt Sara, her mother Maybelle, and her uncle A.P.

In 1951, the Carter Sisters sang backing vocals for gospel singer Carl Smith, and he and June struck up a relationship that led to marriage in 1952 and then a daughter, Rebecca, in 1955. They wrote several songs together, of which the best-known was the bouncy love song "Time's a-Wastin'." Music wasn't her only talent, though. In 1955, director Elia Kazan saw her onstage banter at the Grand Ole Opry and advised her to try acting. She duly went to study at New York's Neighborhood Playhouse and won a few television roles, including in 1957 that of Clarise in the long-running TV western, *Gunsmoke*. The marriage suffered as she continued to work with her mother and sisters, and June later regretted this, saying, "I'm afraid I fell short of what a wife should be . . . If a wife expects to keep her husband she must . . . be a helpmate and forsake mother and father." She and Carl divorced in 1956 and the following year she married Edwin "Rip" Nix, an ex-football player and garage owner with whom she had another daughter, Rosanna.

June became disillusioned with acting after a director lured her to his office late at night on the pretense of it being a casting, and she had to kick him in the shins and run away to avoid being molested. It didn't seem as though stardom was beckoning any day soon, so when Johnny Cash asked if she would like to tour with him, it seemed like a good idea. She made her debut with him in December 1961 and was a great asset from the start. She could play several instruments: guitar, banjo, autoharp, and harmonica; she could write songs (his 1963 hit "Ring of Fire" was by her and a cowriter); she sang harmony; and she also honed a comedy routine that could be used as a warmup. Typically, he would tease her about being three years older than him and she'd fire back with a smart-aleck answer about "the number of miles" he had on him. Before long "Junebug," as he called her, was indispensable to Johnny.

BELOW
A poster for a 1967 show in Minneapolis, when Johnny's addiction was at its worst. "I'd talk to the demons and they'd talk back to me—and I could hear them," he said.

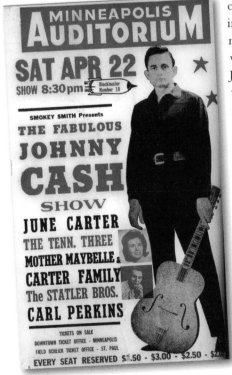

A bottleful of trouble

June and Johnny hadn't been working together long when
she realized that he had a problem—and it came in a pill bottle.
Back in 1957 he had started taking amphetamines (or "speed")
to make him less shy about performing and to boost his energy
onstage. Before long, he needed ever-higher doses to get the
same effect and they stopped him sleeping at night, so he took
sedatives to come down. The handfuls of uppers and downers
he swallowed daily made him irritable and unpredictable—"like
a sunny day or completely dark," according to a friend. When
he was high he would trash hotel rooms, and once smashed
the spotlights on stage at the Grand Ole Opry, showering the
audience with broken glass. Infamously, he caused a huge
forest fire that decimated an endangered colony of Californian
condors when oil dripped into a broken wheel on his truck
and a spark set it alight. Johnny went fishing rather than
attempting to put out the fire or alert the authorities. Vivian
tried to make him come off the pills but he largely sidelined
her, installing her in a California mansion in which to bring up
their four daughters but rarely visiting. His pill consumption

ABOVE
*"I was never looking
back in regret," June
said later. "I never
thought 'Oh, why
didn't I become an
actress?' or 'Why did I
just go paddling after
John?' I've always
walked along right
by his side, and he's
always supported
everything I do."*

"I'M FALLING IN LOVE WITH SOMEONE I HAVE NO RIGHT TO FALL IN LOVE WITH"

increased until he was taking up to a hundred a day, including one known as the "LA Turnaround" because it could reportedly keep truck drivers awake during a trip from New York to Los Angeles and back again.

Despite being aware of his addiction problems, June still couldn't stop herself falling for Johnny, later writing in her autobiography that the attraction started way back in 1961. "I'm falling in love with someone I have no right to fall in love with," she said. She was a deeply religious woman who claimed that at the age of fourteen she had seen tongues of fire and felt the Holy Spirit enter her body. It was against all her religious principles to fall for a married man. She felt bad for Vivian, bad for Rip, and she was scared for Johnny's health—but she simply had to be with him.

Getting clean(-ish)

Johnny rented an apartment in Nashville to be close to June but he was hopeless domestically so she was there the whole time clearing up, ironing his shirts, and flushing any pills she could find down the toilet. For a long time the relationship was unconsummated because of their religious principles, but they grew ever-closer. He wanted to divorce Vivian but at first she refused to let him go, and June said she wouldn't marry him till he got himself off the pills—but that wasn't going to be easy. His whole system relied on them by this stage and it might have been dangerous simply to quit. Meanwhile, his stage performances were going downhill as he slurred the words and became sluggish and unreliable. June and Maybelle persuaded him to see a psychiatrist, to whom he admitted that he had never got over his brother Jack's death and they realized it must be a contributing factor in his addiction. In 1967 he bought a beautiful big house on a lakeside in Hendersonville, north of Nashville, but nearly killed himself after driving a tractor into the lake. At last, when he found himself one day scrabbling around in his garden looking for a hidden stash of pills, he knew he had reached rock bottom. He took off to a cave complex, known as Nickajack Cave, and, in his words, "let God take me from this earth and put me wherever He puts people

OPPOSITE
Johnny traditionally started his concerts by saying, "Hello, I'm Johnny Cash." The songs of his later career, delivered in his deep, distinctive voice, were all about sin and redemption, sorrow and pain.

like me." It wasn't exactly a suicide attempt, but he crawled deep into the mountainside on his own without any idea how he would get back out again, staying up there for hours experiencing his own personal religious epiphany. When he finally got home, June and Maybelle were waiting for him and they set up a round-the-clock team to wean him gradually off the pills. They fed him healthy food and his weight, which had dropped to 140 pounds, rose to 200 again, a much healthier level for a man of 6' 1". By January 1968, Johnny was free of amphetamines and gave a career-defining performance of the song "Folsom Prison Blues" inside the prison itself, an event that was broadcast on TV.

"FOLSOM PRISON BLUES"

Folsom Prison was the second-oldest maximum-security prison in California and the governor ran a tight ship, but a tradition existed of country musicians playing gigs in prisons and in 1966 Johnny was given permission to do a show there. The atmosphere was so electric that he vowed to return and film a concert there, finally persuading CBS to send a film crew with him in January 1968. Two thousand prisoners flocked into the prison dining room, where tables and chairs were nailed to the floor, and Johnny took to the stage. Drug-raddled and swearing, he seemed like one of them. He'd been in jail a few times, for possession of narcotics or drunk driving, although never for more than a night at a time. The performance was raw and edgy, and there were funny moments, such as when Johnny said, without thinking, "This microphone's got a screw loose . . . Can someone come and screw the microphone?" The most moving moment came when he played a song called "Greystone Chapel" that had been written by an inmate named Glen Sherley. When it aired, the film introduced Johnny to a new young set of fans, who saw him as ultra-cool.

Vivian finally let Johnny have his divorce after falling
for someone else herself, and in February 1968, during a
concert in London, Ontario, in front of 5,000 people, Johnny
proposed to June. She hesitated while the audience yelled
encouragement until at last she agreed, to great cheers and
applause. The wedding took place on March 1, and afterward
they threw a party for 150 people. June was determined to be
a traditional wife this time so that her third marriage would
last the course: "If he wants me to work, I work, and if he
wants me to wash dishes, I wash dishes." They prayed and
studied the Bible and Johnny rededicated his life to God,
making lots of gospel records and becoming good friends
with the famous evangelical preacher Billy Graham. Their
son John was born in 1970.

Johnny's part of the deal was to stay off pills—and he
managed it for long periods, but he was always at risk. When
he went to play for American troops in Vietnam in 1969 a
doctor gave him Dexedrine (a form of speed) to combat jetlag
and straightaway he was hooked again. June realized the minute
he got back and nagged him into quitting once more. He was
clean for seven years from 1970, but a relapse in the late '70s
led to a rocky patch in their marriage. They got through it
and renewed their wedding vows in 1979, but in 1981 he was
attacked by an ostrich they kept on their land, causing serious
abdominal injuries and triggering another relapse into pill-
popping and erratic behavior. During a stay in hospital after
injuring his hand ripping up a hotel room in
England, Johnny took his own pills on top of
the ones the hospital doled out and nearly
ended up in a coma. In 1983 the family
checked him into the Betty
Ford Center to detox, but it
wouldn't be the last time he
slipped up. "Drugs, they'll
sneak up on you," he told
a reporter. "All of a
sudden there'll be
a beautiful little
Percodan lying
there and you'll

BELOW
June and Johnny with
little John in 1967.
Johnny was smitten by
his new son and wanted
to be the kind of father
that he'd failed to be for
his daughters.

want it." The last twenty years of his life were marked by periods when he was clean and others when he fell off the wagon. It was what Johnny called a "family disease," with two of his sisters, two brothers, and most of his children affected by addictions.

Somehow June put up with it. They bought a house in Jamaica where they could relax, and gradually spent more time there after Johnny stopped touring. He suffered from poor health in his final years and loved ones feared for his future, but then in 2003, in a twist of fate, June unexpectedly succumbed to complications following a routine heart operation and passed away at the age of seventy-three. Johnny was grief-stricken. He'd hoped for many more years with her and found it hard to carry on without the "soft, fluffy Mama bear" who looked after him with her heart and soul. She had made him promise he would keep working if she died first and he obeyed, recording over fifty songs in the next four months before dying himself.

He'd put June through a lot over the years but she never turned her back on him when most other women would have thrown in the towel. He was her Johnny, the man she described as "probably the most unusual, fine, unselfish person I've known."

"DRUGS, THEY'LL SNEAK UP ON YOU"

ABOVE
In his autobiography, Johnny wrote, "June said she knew me, knew the kernel of me, deep inside, beneath the drugs and deceit and despair and anger and selfishness, and she knew my loneliness."

"EVERYBODY LIKED IKE, PRETTY MUCH."
HE MUST HAVE HAD A WAY WITH WOMEN

IKE
&
TINA
TURNER

ROCK 'N' ROLL

IKE WISTER TURNER

Born: November 5, 1931
Clarksdale, Mississippi

Died: December 12, 2007
San Marcos, California

ANNA MAE BULLOCK

Born: November 26, 1939
Nutbush, Tennessee

Married: 1962
Tijuana, Mexico
(not legal)

Little Anna Mae was just seventeen when she grabbed a mike and sang for Ike Turner, the charismatic leader of the Kings of Rhythm. He was a Svengali figure who would soon reinvent her as Tina Turner, and she couldn't help falling in love with him. Until, that is, she became his prisoner . . .

Ike grew up in the South at a time of segregation, when African-Americans were supposed to keep to their own areas, and someone would most likely "teach them a lesson" if they didn't. He was just three when his father was beaten up by a white gang leader and so badly injured that when he was thrown into his front yard, Ike saw the holes kicked in his stomach. He died two years later as a result of those injuries. Ike's mother remarried but the new stepfather was an alcoholic who was violent toward the boy. It appears this was not the only abuse he suffered, as he would later claim that a local woman sexually abused him from the age of six. Casual sex and violence appear to have been endemic in the Mississippi of his youth, and this had its effects on him as he grew up—he always carried a gun, and he went through women like other people go through cups of coffee. "It was like he was a magnet," says a guitarist he used to work with. "There were five or six women a day."

> **"IKE WAS A MAGNET ... THERE WERE FIVE OR SIX WOMEN A DAY"**

Music was Ike's passion and his salvation. From the age of eight he began hanging around the local radio station, WROX, where they played blues records. According to Ike, the DJs let him put records on when they slipped out for a break, and "that was the beginning of my thing with music." He was given a job at the station and began to play music himself: he took up piano after hearing blues pianist Pinetop Perkins, and he taught himself to play guitar by listening to blues records and emulating the sound. At high school he started his first band, the Tophatters, covering big-band numbers. When the Tophatters broke up, Ike formed the Kings of Rhythm, playing boogie-woogie and blues, and they began to get regular gigs in the Clarksville area, as well as airplay on the local radio stations. Ike was a likable guy, who made friends in the business and was invited to play with other blues artists, including Muddy Waters, Elmore James, and

OPPOSITE
There was no question Tina was the star right from the start, but music company executive Robert Johnson believed that Ike "had the capacity to cast a spell on people with his music that emoted power no one could resist."

Howlin' Wolf. Shows could last for twelve hours at a stretch, so when one guy needed to use the bathroom, another would step in and play his instrument.

In 1951, Ike and the band wrote the song "Rocket 88." The band's saxophonist Jackie Brenston sang the vocals, they recorded it, and signed it over to a record company who went on to sell half a million copies of the song. There are many who now claim "Rocket 88" as the first genuine rock 'n' roll record but at the time Ike received no recognition. In fact, he was disgusted that the company released it under the name of Jackie Brenston and his Delta Cats instead of the Kings of Rhythm; having written the intro and the first verse, he considered it more his song than anyone else's. As with much of his later musical career, Ike felt he was the one in the background doing the work while others got the credit. It was a pattern that kept repeating, as it did in 1956 when he brought Anna Mae Bullock up on stage to sing with the Kings of Rhythm—it was obvious from the start that she was the star of the show. Given subsequent events, it could be easy to dismiss Ike as some guy who rode to success on her coattails but in fact his contribution to blues music back in the '50s and '60s was

BELOW
Ike ran a tight ship, fining band members for minor misdemeanors like shoes that weren't shined or a fastener missing on a dress. It was possible for them to owe him money at the end of a tour.

substantial. But that was all back in the days before he started boozing and doing drugs. Teetotal till the age of thirty, once he discovered the lure of the white powder, everything would begin to change.

A teenage single mom

Racial tensions in 1940s Nutbush, Tennessee, weren't as fraught as they had been in 1930s Mississippi. Anna Mae grew up friends with some of the white families in the area, where her father was the overseer on a white man's farm, although she says, "It was almost by intuition that you knew the nice white people from the bad ones, and when to really stay clear." World War II disrupted her childhood, with both parents going off to work for the war effort, leaving her in the care of her paternal grandmother. He introduced her to the Pentecostal church, where she sang the music she loved. After the war she moved back in with her parents, but her father was violent and when she was eleven her mother ran away to escape him. This made the young Anna Mae feel as though she "wasn't wanted," and two years later when her father went off with a younger woman, she was sent to live with her maternal grandmother.

When her grandmother died, Anna Mae moved to St. Louis to live with her mother and her sister Alline, and the girls began to hang around the clubs where live bands played. Anna Mae was just sixteen when Alline took her to Club Manhattan to see the Kings of Rhythm with Ike Turner, the band leader all the girls wanted. "I wonder why so many women like him?" Anna Mae asked. "He sure is ugly." But she was keen to get a chance to sing with the band, so one evening, during an intermission when Ike was adjusting the instruments on stage, she grabbed a mike and began to sing a B. B. King song. Her voice was extraordinary—very rich and

COCAINE

Coke has often been the rock star's drug of choice, perhaps because it tends to enhance stage performances by making users more alert and energetic, unlike marijuana and heroin, which dull the senses, or mind-altering LSD. Aside from Ike Turner, among the stars who have admitted to indulging in an excess of cocaine are Elton John, Keith Richards, and Eric Clapton. John Entwistle of The Who, considered by many to be the best rock bass guitarist of all time, died in 2002 of a massive heart attack brought on by cocaine use, and there have almost certainly been other cocaine-related rock-star deaths which coroners reported simply as heart attacks. J. J. Cale wrote the song "Cocaine" about the drug in 1977, which Eric Clapton made famous in a cover version. Although the message of the lyrics is that cocaine can keep you going if you've run out of steam or cheer you up if depressed, the repetition and tone of the song make it an antidrugs anthem.

powerful—and Ike instantly hired her. Her mother was furious when she found out, because Anna Mae was still at school and Ike had a terrible reputation, but in fact it was the saxophone player Raymond Hill she got involved with, and in November 1957 she found out she was pregnant with his child. They talked about marriage but he disappeared before the baby was born, so at the age of eighteen, Anna Mae became a single mom.

There wasn't much money in singing for Kings of Rhythm so during the day Anna Mae worked as a nursing assistant and by night she sang, and gradually she and Ike became "like brother and sister." He taught her about music and helped to develop her range. If only it had stayed that way, all could have worked out fine. Instead, in a period when he had broken up with his latest wife, Lorraine, Ike seduced Anna Mae. It felt wrong to her, like incest or something similar, but soon she found herself falling in love with him. Back in those days, as Tina later said, "Everybody liked Ike, pretty much." He must have had a way with women. As one former girlfriend put it, "Once you go to bed with him, you want to stick around."

WHILE SEPARATED FROM HIS WIFE, IKE SEDUCED ANNA MAE

Under his thumb

Ike had a casual attitude toward the women in his life, just as he had a casual attitude to marriage. No one knows for sure how many times he married; he claims fourteen in his autobiography, but many of those would have been bigamous. He had at least six children by three different women, and possibly a number of unacknowledged ones. When Anna Mae also found herself pregnant with his child at the end of January 1960, he went straight back to his previous wife while continuing to see her on the side. In the meantime, he insisted she keep working right through the pregnancy, wearing support garments to hide her bulge. During this period, he made a recording of her singing a song called "Fool in Love" and sent it out to record companies. Juggy Murray of the New York label Sue was crazy about it and soon called them into the recording studio. The track was released under the names "Ike and Tina Turner" after Ike coined a new name for her, and the

single made number two in
the R&B charts—Ike's most
successful track to date. Tina
didn't see any money from it,
though. Ike paid her rent but
kept the rest, and when she
dared to say she didn't think it
could work out between them
because they were "two totally
different people," he beat her
for the first time, attacking her
viciously with a shoe stretcher

with a metal rod down the middle. She was pregnant with his
child and utterly terrified. She knew she should leave but she
needed him to pay the bills; she also loved the new career he
was helping to forge for her—and she loved him, too. That
night she decided she would stay while trying to find a way
to make things better.

Their child, Ronald Renelle, was born in October 1960,
with Tina still performing on stage just two days before the
birth, and then again not long afterward. Lorraine left when

ABOVE
The opening of Bolic
Studios, Ike's empire
HQ, in Inglewood, 1971.
He had closed-circuit
television cameras
everywhere so he could
spy on employees—
including Tina.

BELOW
Tina on stage at
Madison Square Garden,
1969, when she and Ike
were opening for The
Rolling Stones. She
taught Mick Jagger
some dance moves.

ABOVE
Tina at home with her son Ronnie Renelle Turner. When he was born, she said, "Ike was nowhere around, of course."

she saw how much the baby looked like Ike; up till then he'd denied having an affair with Tina, but the resemblance was too great. His behavior became increasingly controlling and unpredictable during this period. In 1960 he'd started taking cocaine, and by the end of the decade he was heavily addicted; he later told a journalist that by the early '70s he was spending $56,000 a month on it and by 1974 he had worn a hole in his nasal septum. The cocaine made him violent for no reason, and Tina says, "You never knew when you were going to get it—or why." He beat her with shoes, shoe trees, or his fists. "I always had a cut on my head somewhere, always had bruises." Ike had been brought up in a world where men hit their women and he didn't see anything wrong with what he was doing: "Yeah, I hit her," he admitted, "But I didn't hit her more than the average guy beats his wife." In the early years Tina remained hopeful that things would change, so in 1962 when Ike asked her to marry him, she agreed. They drove down to Tijuana in Mexico, saw a sign by the roadside that said "Marriage," and went into a dusty, dirty building where a guy shoved a piece of paper at them; they both signed and that was it—or so Tina believed at the time. In fact, Ike was still married to someone else whom he didn't divorce until 1974, so their marriage was never legal.

Throughout their relationship, Ike slept with dozens of other women: some were long-term affairs with women in the band or its backup team, while others were just girls passing in the night. Tina gave up counting, simply requesting (in vain) that he didn't do it in their bed. She focused on bringing up her two sons, as well as two of Ike's sons from a previous relationship, and working on her music. And gradually, very gradually, she realized that she might be able to have a career in the industry without Ike, as one by one big-name musicians called to ask if they could work with her.

The long road to freedom

In 1965, Phil Spector, a producer known for creating a "Wall of Sound" in his tracks, invited Tina to record a song called "River Deep—Mountain High." The fee was $25,000, his only stipulation being that Ike mustn't be allowed in the studio, as he didn't want any interference. Although the track wasn't a hit in the US when first released, it made a big impression on many who heard it, with Beatle George Harrison calling it "a perfect record from start to finish." Then in 1966, Ike and Tina were invited to support The Rolling Stones during a tour of the UK, which greatly raised their profile, and they went on to support more Stones tours in both Europe and the US. In 1971, Tina won a Grammy award for Best R&B Vocal Performance for a track called "Proud Mary," and in 1973 she wrote a hit song herself, "Nutbush City Limits," a track about her old hometown. Then in 1975, she acted in her first movie role as the Acid Queen *Tommy*. There was no question that her career was on the up.

She often went to fortune-tellers, who told her that one day she would be a big star without Ike, but her self-esteem had been so destroyed by the relationship she found it hard to

LEFT
Ike and Tina. "At first I had really been in love with him," she later admitted in her autobiography. "Look what he'd done for me. But he was too unpredictable."

41

ROCK STARS IN THE MOVIES

In the 1975 movie *Tommy*, based on the rock opera by The Who, Tina was majestic as the Acid Queen, a prostitute dealing in LSD. In *Mad Max Beyond Thunderdome* (1985) she played a ruthless Amazonian type clad in an extraordinary chainmail costume. Neither role stretched her as an actress but reflected her on-stage image as a tough woman wearing sexy leathers and belting out her hits. Movie producers often cast rock stars in roles that are extensions of their public image: David Bowie playing an alien in *The Man Who Fell to Earth* (1976); Mick Jagger an eccentric rock star involved in a ménage à trois in *Performance* (1970); or Bob Geldof as a rock star losing his mind in *Pink Floyd The Wall* (1982). However, Bob Dylan played against type as a knife-wielding killer in *Pat Garrett and Billy the Kid* (1972); Cher has proved herself an accomplished actress in many roles, winning an Oscar for *Moonstruck* (1987); and, more recently, Björk gave an acclaimed performance as a woman going blind in *Dancer in the Dark* (2000). Rock stars' success, or otherwise, in movies is partly about talent, but more about intelligent casting and a decent script.

believe. She was his prisoner, scared of his threats and too insecure to take a stand against him. On one occasion he broke her jaw right before a show, forcing her to go on stage and perform with her mouth swollen and bleeding. After that she took an overdose of Valium, but was rushed to hospital to have her stomach pumped. "I just wanna die," she told Ike when he came to her bedside—but instead he forced her straight back to work.

A turning point came when Tina discovered Nichiren Shōshū Buddhism. She began to chant regularly and found it made her stronger and more focused, helping her to "rearrange her place in the universe." And then on July 4, 1976, Ike beat her up in the car on the way to a gig and suddenly enough was enough. She slipped away from the venue before the concert and made her escape with just 36 cents in her purse. Ike stalked her to the friends' houses where she stayed, and did all he could to force her back, but her mind was made up and she

sued for divorce. Nothing deterred her, not even when she found she was liable for reimbursing all the promoters of the canceled tour dates.

Tina needed to make money to support her sons and herself, and she still wanted to sing. It was then she discovered how much she was respected by her peers in the music industry as big stars flocked to help. Mick Jagger invited her on the 1981 Stones tour and brought her on stage to duet with him on "Honky Tonk Women;" Rod Stewart did a duet of "Hot Legs" with her on *Saturday Night Live*; David Bowie let her sing his number "1984;" and Mark Knopfler of Dire Straits gave her the song "Private Dancer." Olivia Newton John, Chuck Berry, Al Green, Keith Richards, Ron Wood—dozens of musicians helped her, and the 1984 album *Private Dancer,* featuring the single "What's Love Got to Do With It?," was a huge success. Her days of scraping around for money were over.

ABOVE
In his 1999 autobiography, Taking Back My Name, *Ike attempted to defend his reputation. "I've slapped Tina," he admitted, "but I've never beaten her."*

Ike, on the other hand, went into freefall without her, especially after his name was blackened by her warts-and-all 1986 autobiography. He was arrested several times in the '80s for drugs and firearm offenses, and spent eighteen months in jail in 1990/91—a period which at least helped him to get free of his cocaine habit. He married again, to singer Jeanette Bazelle, and had more musical successes, but in 2007 he died of emphysema after succumbing yet again to addiction. Tina became one of the greatest female artists of all time, winning eight Grammy awards and selling 100 million singles and albums worldwide. In 1986 she found love with German record producer Erwin Bach and in 2013 the couple married near their home in Switzerland. When Ike died, Tina was approached by the press for a comment, but her spokesperson simply said that they had not had any contact in thirty years and she had nothing more to add.

OPPOSITE
Her own woman at last—Tina in 1984 promoting Private Dancer, *the solo album from which there would be seven hit singles. Her voice "melts vinyl" said an* LA Times *reviewer.*

ELVIS PRESLEY

&

PRISCILLA BEAULIEU

ROCK 'N' ROLL

ELVIS AARON
PRESLEY

Born: January 8, 1935
Tupelo, Mississippi

Died: August 16, 1977
Memphis, Tennessee

PRISCILLA BEAULIEU
(BORN WAGNER)

Born: May 24, 1945
Brooklyn, New York

Married: May 1, 1967
Las Vegas, Nevada

It might seem strange that when she was fourteen Priscilla's parents let her date a twenty-four-year-old, and stranger still that when she was seventeen they let her fly to the States to stay in his house with him. But this wasn't any young man—this was Elvis Presley, the King of Rock 'n' Roll.

★

Priscilla was upset when her family moved from Texas to Wiesbaden in Germany in 1956. It meant yet another change of school for the rather shy young girl, her sixth to date because of her father's army career, and she was homesick. She took to hanging out at the town's Eagles Club where she could listen to music on the jukebox and write letters to friends back home. One day in spring 1959 when she was there with her brother, a man came over and introduced himself as Currie Grant. "How would you like to meet Elvis?" he asked. Priscilla wasn't an obsessive Elvis fan, like some of her classmates, but she thought he was very handsome and was aware he was doing his national service nearby. Currie Grant and his wife took her along to the three-story house in Bad Nauheim where Elvis was having a party. After much agonizing she had decided to wear a navy-and-white sailor dress. A sign on the front gate read, in German: "Autographs between 7 and 8 p.m. only," but there were still some girls hanging around though by now it was after 8. Priscilla's first impression of Elvis was that "He was handsomer than he appeared in films, younger and more vulnerable-looking with his GI haircut." He asked her what year she was in at school and when she replied he exclaimed, "Ninth grade? Why, you're just a baby." She felt foolish, but enjoyed it when he sat down at the piano and played and sang, making her laugh with his Jerry Lee Lewis impersonation.

OPPOSITE
"Presley is a definite danger to the security of the United States . . . [His] actions and motions are such as to arouse the sexual passions of the teenaged youth," wrote the staff of a Catholic newspaper in Wisconsin to FBI director J. Edgar Hoover in 1956.

BELOW
When asked by Time *magazine in May 1956 if he would marry, Elvis replied, "Why buy a cow when you can get milk through the fence?"*

ABOVE
Priscilla was photographed waving goodbye to Elvis as he left Germany on March 2, 1960. The pictures were reproduced in LIFE *magazine.*

To her surprise, he asked if he could see her again. "You're refreshing," he told her. "It's nice to talk to someone from back home. It gets a little lonely here." His mother Gladys, the person he was closest to in the world, had died soon after he arrived in Germany. "She would have liked you," Elvis told Priscilla sadly.

Her parents were worried about her visiting this man ten years her senior, so Elvis visited her father wearing his army uniform and, addressing him as "Captain Beaulieu," explained that he would take good care of his daughter and ensure they were chaperoned at all times. Her father agreed they could continue to see each other and the visits became regular events at which they talked, laughed, and had a kiss and a cuddle—but that was all. Just six months later, in March 1960, Elvis flew back to the United States promising to keep in touch. Priscilla was heartbroken as he walked away into the airport, but she would have been even more upset if she'd realized she wouldn't see him again for two whole years.

He called, but not as often as she would have liked. She wept when she read in gossip magazines that he had a girlfriend called Anita Wood and that he'd also been dating Nancy Sinatra, the daughter of Frank. The days dragged past, and she lived from phone call to phone call, then in March 1962 came the call that changed everything: "I haven't been able to put you out of my mind," Elvis said, and invited her to visit him at Graceland, his home in Memphis. She begged and pleaded with her parents to be allowed to go. They set a long list of conditions, to which Elvis agreed, and just after her seventeenth birthday, Priscilla flew off on her own for a two-week visit to the most famous rock 'n' roll star on the planet.

Sergeant Presley & Colonel Parker

Elvis was the only child of a young Mississippi couple, Gladys and Vernon Presley. Vernon drifted between jobs and they were often forced to ask family or neighbors to help put food on the table. Elvis had a strong bond with his mother, a religious woman who took him to a gospel-singing church that would be his earliest musical influence. They grew up in an African-American area and Elvis liked listening to the Mississippi Slim show on the radio, featuring rhythm-and-blues songs. He

ELVIS HAD DECIDED HE WANTED TO BE A BIG STAR AND PURSUED HIS DREAMS WITH FIERCE DETERMINATION

was given a guitar one Christmas and began taking lessons from a neighbor. At high school he stood out from his peers with his long sideburns, carefully oiled hair, and almost effeminate good looks. By the time he graduated Elvis had decided he wanted to be a big star and pursued his dreams with fierce determination. He got a lucky break when he met Sam Phillips at the small Sun Records label. Sam had been saying for a while that he would like to find a white man who could sing like an African-American. In 1954 he helped Elvis to cut a single called "That's All Right," and when this was played on the radio, callers to the station were convinced it was sung by a black man on account of the rich, soulful vocals. It sold 20,000 copies.

BELOW
Elvis, aged about ten, with his mother and father. He said about Gladys, "She was the most wonderful mother anyone could ever have."

Elvis threw himself into live shows, in which he developed his trademark leg gyrations and pelvic thrusts, leading the New York *Daily News* critic to comment that he "gave an exhibition that was suggestive and vulgar, tinged with the kind of animalism that should be confined to dives and bordellos." The girls loved it, and soon he had hordes of screaming fans at every gig. By 1956 he was riding high, with frequent TV appearances combined with a string of five singles that reached number one in the charts, including "Heartbreak Hotel," "Hound Dog," and "Love Me Tender." In March that year he signed up shrewd musical impresario Colonel Tom Parker as his manager, a move that secured his future. And then, just

THE ROOTS OF ROCK 'N' ROLL

The word "roll" had long had sexual connotations, from phrases such as "a roll in the hay," and by the early 20th century, "rock" was being used by African-Americans as a slang term for rhythm-and-blues music. The two terms merged to mean "dancing in a suggestive fashion"—or simply to have sex, as in the 1922 song title "My Man Rocks Me (With One Steady Roll)." Rock 'n' roll music, a combination of rhythm and blues, swing, boogie-woogie, gospel, country, and folk, emerged in the early to mid-1950s. It was generally played with one or two electric guitars, a blues-style rhythm, and a backbeat provided by a snare drum. The 45 rpm vinyl record had just come on sale, at prices that teenagers could afford, and rock 'n' roll became wildly popular almost overnight. Some rock historians claim that the first rock 'n' roll record was "Rocket 88," sung by Jackie Brenston, recorded in 1951, but the first major hit was Bill Haley's "Rock Around the Clock," released on May 20, 1954. Elvis quickly followed with "That's All Right," which came out on July 19 that year.

RIGHT
Elvis recorded "You're a Heartbreaker" in December 1954, at Memphis's famous Sun Studios.

when everything was going stellar, Elvis received his call-up papers for a two-year stint of national service. It was a devastating blow. He was terrified the fans would forget all about him during a two-year absence, but before he set off Colonel Parker made him record some singles that were then released strategically every few months to keep him in the public eye.

In March 1958, Elvis started training at Fort Hood, Texas, and in October he was shipped over to Germany, leaving behind a heartbroken girlfriend, Anita Wood, whom he'd been dating since the previous year. She'd been about to sign a contract as an actress with Paramount Pictures but gave it up at Elvis's request to be available whenever he wanted to see her. Once he was in Germany, she read in the newspapers about his relationship with Priscilla but when she challenged him on the telephone Elvis assured her Priscilla was just a child he was friendly with, the daughter of an army officer. When he returned to the US in March 1960, the pair resumed their relationship and Anita hoped they would get married, but at the same time she kept finding letters to him from Priscilla. One day she overheard him telling his father that he couldn't choose between Priscilla and Anita—so she told him she would make the decision for him by leaving. It was tough. But she knew she was doing the right thing.

Coming to Graceland

Priscilla loved Elvis with all the fervor of a schoolgirl's first crush. She visited Graceland in summer 1962, then again for Christmas when Elvis gave her a puppy, which she named Honey. He spoke to her father and somehow persuaded him that Priscilla should come and stay with his father and stepmother to finish high school at a local Memphis school. Her parents were wary because they didn't like the way Elvis was influencing their daughter, making her dye her hair jet black and tease it into a beehive hairstyle, and rimming her eyes with heavy black eyeliner, but she refused to settle back at school in Germany because she pined for him so much. Elvis promised to make sure she graduated from high school and that they were chaperoned at all times, so in the end they agreed. Priscilla moved over and soon she was spending every night in Elvis's bed. They fooled around but he would not have full sex with her, saying that sex was special and he wanted it to happen at the perfect moment. He installed a go-kart track at Graceland on which they could race around, and they enjoyed pillow fights, swimming in the pool, and listening to music on his poolside jukebox.

When Elvis was away from home, Priscilla was consumed with loneliness and worry that he would meet someone else,

BELOW
Elvis bought Graceland in 1957 and turned it into his sanctuary. Among the twenty-three rooms, there was a basement viewing room with three television sets and a wet bar, and a Jungle Room with green shag carpet and Hawaiian-style decor.

and her worst fears were justified when he had an affair with Swedish-American actress Ann-Margret while filming *Viva Las Vegas* (1964). Ann-Margret announced to the press that they were engaged, but when Priscilla confronted Elvis he blamed the media for spreading unsubstantiated rumors. Still, every time he worked with a new leading lady Priscilla was knotted up with jealousy. By this time, she knew Elvis took prescription drugs to get to sleep, to give him energy, and to help him lose weight, because he often gave her some too. She had learned that he had fluctuating moods, and bursts of temper when things weren't going his own way. But she responded with utter loyalty and devotion, trying to pre-empt his bad moods and be his ideal woman in every way.

Just before Christmas 1966, Elvis presented Priscilla with a diamond engagement ring. Some speculate that her father might have put pressure on him to propose, while others believe that Colonel Parker encouraged him to make an honest woman of her since he had a morals clause in his contract with his record company. Priscilla was delighted; it was her dream come true. Their wedding in Las Vegas was closely stage-managed by Colonel Parker, with a brief stop at the city clerk's office, a small ceremony in the Aladdin Hotel from which most of their friends were excluded, then a flight back to their Los Angeles home on Frank Sinatra's private jet. Elvis was nervous on their wedding night, Priscilla said later, but at last he "made a woman of her"—and she got pregnant almost immediately because he had instructed her not to take birth control pills. She was upset about the pregnancy, scared of losing him because before they married he had once told her that he could never make love to a woman who'd

BELOW
Elvis and Priscilla with Lisa Marie. "I wanted to create a home. I wanted to have children. I wanted him to be a husband," she said later. But "it was never going to be that way. It couldn't be that way."

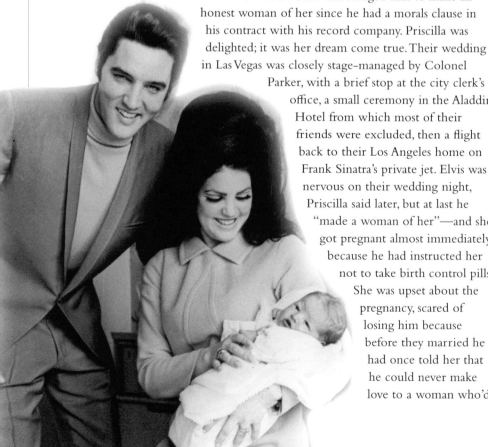

had a baby. Elvis was delighted when their daughter Lisa Marie was born in February 1968. He loved playing with the baby—but it was months before he made love to Priscilla again, and from then on their love-making became more and more infrequent. He treated her like his sister, his playmate, but not like a lover.

> # HE TREATED HER LIKE HIS SISTER, HIS PLAYMATE, BUT NOT LIKE A LOVER

Friends for life

Elvis had always made it clear to Priscilla that he didn't want her to work: "It's either me or a career, Baby," he said. "Because when I call you, I need you to be there." But he was away from home for long periods and wouldn't let her accompany him. Wives and girlfriends weren't allowed on tour, and he certainly didn't want her hanging around and cramping his style on movie sets. By the late 1960s his career was in the doldrums as he hadn't had a number one hit since 1962 and he hated the movie roles he was being offered in cheesy musicals with predictable plots. He took more and more pills and she found him unreachable even when he was back in Graceland. Priscilla took dance lessons to try and fill her time and had a brief affair with her dance instructor, which only served to demonstrate all the passion that was missing in her marriage. Then in 1972, Elvis introduced her to a karate instructor called Mike Stone, suggesting she should take karate lessons. He had learned karate while in Germany and was a keen advocate. Priscilla began her lessons and before long was having an affair with Mike, which quickly became serious. When she told Elvis about it he threw her down on the bed and made love to her roughly, saying, "This is how a real man makes love to his woman." For her it was the last straw, and she told him she wanted a divorce.

Elvis was distraught about the breakup—some friends say it was "a blow from which he never recovered." He raged against Stone and considered organizing a contract killing but saw sense before going through with it. He was determined that he and Priscilla should remain friends, so they held hands throughout the 1973 divorce hearing and stayed in frequent contact by telephone afterward. Priscilla was shocked whenever she saw him, though: his face was swollen and his figure was

LISA MARIE & MICHAEL JACKSON

Priscilla Presley was openly disapproving when in 1994 her daughter, Lisa Marie, announced that she was marrying pop superstar Michael Jackson. She wondered if this was an attempt by Lisa Marie somehow to connect with her famous father, there being many similarities between the two. Both Michael and Elvis were legendary stars who led privileged, reclusive lives; both had a childlike side and surrounded themselves with crowds of sycophants; and both had addictions to prescription drugs (although Lisa Marie didn't know this about Jackson at the time of their wedding). Media speculation abounded that the union was a fraud, arriving just as Jackson was accused of molesting a young boy, but Lisa Marie insists that the marriage was intimate in every sense. She says they divorced two years later partly because he was pressuring her to have a child and she didn't feel ready for it, and also because she was worried about his health. They continued to see each other on and off for four years after the divorce, and she was devastated when, in 2009, in what must have seemed like history repeating itself, she heard the news of his premature death from a prescription drug overdose.

badly bloated. On stage, he was forgetting lyrics and had almost become a figure of ridicule, with his rhinestone-studded costumes and long fringed jackets. There were a couple of girlfriends—Linda Thompson and Ginger Alden—but neither relationship was consummated. It is possible the effects of so many prescription drugs had made him impotent.

Early in 1977, Priscilla and Elvis chatted on the phone and speculated that maybe they had met too young, and perhaps they would get back together when she was sixty and he was seventy, when they could race around in golf carts. She visited him one last time after that, then on August 16 she got a call from Elvis's road manager to tell her he was dead, having suffered a massive heart attack that was probably brought on by his years of prescription drug abuse compounded by his obesity. The autopsy found "fourteen drugs in his system, ten in significant quantity." Priscilla said that "the sun went out" with his death. She still loved him with a "deep and abiding love" and cites him as the greatest influence in her life.

LEFT
Elvis often spoke out against illegal street drugs but never worried about his dependence on excessive numbers of prescription drugs because they were all authorized by doctors. He struggled to control his weight but his favorite foods were the fried ones of his Southern roots.

Theirs had been a strong but curiously sexless relationship that lasted fourteen years altogether. It may be that Elvis was insecure around women his own age, prompting him to choose a young girl he could try to mold into the wife he wanted. Perhaps his extraordinarily close relationship with his mother caused him to have what psychologists call a "Madonna/whore" complex that prevented him from becoming sexually aroused within a committed and loving partnership. Priscilla never had any regrets about her marriage to the King of Rock 'n' Roll: "I lived a really wonderful life with this man and even after our divorce, it was incredible," she said. "We realized that we liked each other, and that's very special."

OPPOSITE
Lisa Marie was taken to a Michael Jackson concert by her father when she was six years old and Michael was sixteen. They later married in the Dominican Republic on May 26, 1994, but in early 1996, she filed for divorce, citing "irreconcilable differences."

BOB DYLAN
&
JOAN BAEZ

ROCK 'N' ROLL

ROBERT ALLEN ZIMMERMAN

Born: May 24, 1941
Duluth, Minnesota

JOAN CHANDOS BAEZ

Born: January 9, 1941
Staten Island, New York City

⭐

"IT'S FAIR TO SAY I FELL UNDER THAT SPELL OF HIS"

Joan was the Queen of Folk Music, with albums racing up the charts and all her concerts selling out, while Bob struggled to fill a coffeehouse with his shows. A friend suggested, "All you need to do is start screwing Joan Baez. . . . That's your ticket, man." And soon afterward he did.

★

oan's father Albert was born in Puebla, Mexico, but his family moved to Brooklyn when he was ten years old. He studied mathematics and physics at university, and became an eminent professor of physics and the coinventor of the x-ray microscope. Of his three daughters, Joan, the middle one, was perhaps the strongest character although she was insecure about her looks because her skin was darker than that of her pretty younger sister Mimi, and kids at school taunted her, calling her "a dirty Mexican." She had a powerful singing voice and, after seeing a Pete Seeger folk concert at high school aged thirteen, she decided, "I can be a singer too." The family had been living in California but in 1958 they moved to Massachusetts and Joan enrolled at the Massachusetts Institute of Technology. She began to sing in the coffeehouses of Cambridge, and contemporaries were instantly impressed: "she had a voice that would make angels cry," said one, while others spoke of her seeming vulnerability on stage, which was in contrast to the extraordinary sounds she produced. She fell in love with an undergraduate called Michael New and for the first time in her life, Joan said later, she fell "passionately, insanely, and irrationally in love."

At the influential Newport Folk Festival on July 11, 1959, Joan plucked up the courage to sing and the audience went crazy for her. After that she pulled out of university to sing full-time and contributed three songs to an album called *Folksingers 'Round Harvard Square*. A solo album followed in 1960, of which the *New York Times* critic wrote, "At the age of only 20, Miss Baez has truly arrived." She began singing in clubs in New York and it was there, on April 10, 1961, that she first encountered Bob Dylan. She and her sister Mimi attended what was known as

OPPOSITE
Joan's pure soprano and Bob's nasal twang were an odd but powerful mismatch when they sang together.

BELOW
Joan said, "The easiest kind of relationship for me is with ten thousand people. The hardest is with one."

"HE HAD A SILLY CAP ON, AND HE SEEMED LIKE SUCH A LITTLE BOY. BUT HE WAS A JOY TO EXPERIENCE"

"hoot night," basically an open-mike night for any singers in town. Bob performed a couple of numbers and Joan recalled, "He had [a] silly cap on, and he seemed like such a little boy. But he was a joy to experience." He followed her out of the club, asking if she would like to perform his song, "Hey, Woodie," then he turned and invited Mimi to a party. Joan replied sharply that Mimi, who was not yet sixteen, had to get home. But she liked the song—and she was intrigued by him.

Falling under the spell

Contrary to what he would imply to journalists in later years, Robert Zimmerman had a comfortable middle-class upbringing, with a father who ran a furniture and appliance business and a mother who worked in a clerical job. While at school, he performed in a series of garage bands, and at the University of Minnesota he took up electric guitar and began

RIGHT
Joan's guitar playing combined chords with finger plucking to fill out the sound, since she worked without a backing band.

playing at coffee shops under different stage names: Elston Gunn, Bob Dillon, and later Bob Dylan. If anyone asked, he told them he didn't have any parents, or that he had Sioux Indian blood, or that he had run away to join a carnival at the age of thirteen: the variety of colorful tales he span were designed to mislead and signaled his very early desire for privacy—something that would be taken to extremes in later life.

Bob moved to New York and began performing around Greenwich Village in his trademark corduroy cap, jeans, worn-out boots, and stained shirts, playing songs he had written himself. By September 1961, he had signed up with a manager, Albert Grossman, but he wasn't pulling in the crowds. Only fifty-three people attended his concert at the Folklore Center on November 4, whereas the following Saturday Joan played to a sell-out crowd of 1,700 while another 200 had to be turned away. Bob's first album sold poorly, with just 5,000 copies shifted in a year, while Joan's second one, which came out around the same time, got to number 13 in the charts and kept on selling for two years. It wasn't for lack of trying: Bob had already written some great songs, such as "Blowin' in the Wind" and "The Times They Are a-Changin'," but they tended to do better when covered by other people. Several songs were inspired by Suze Rotolo, an Italian girl who worked for the Congress of Racial Equality, whom he began dating soon after he arrived in New York. In his memoirs, he wrote of her: "Cupid's arrow had whistled past my ears before but this time it hit me in the heart and the weight of it dragged me overboard."

While Bob was still struggling to establish himself, Joan was already finding the pressures of fame wearisome and she moved to a cabin in the Carmel Highlands of California where she could relax and consider her future. Her family were Quakers and she always knew she wanted her music to help promote social justice and peace. "There was no question about the

THE FOLKLORE CENTER
Presents

BOB DYLAN
IN HIS FIRST NEW YORK CONCERT

SAT. NOV. 4, 1961   8:40pm

CARNEGIE CHAPTER HALL
154 WEST 57th STREET • NEW YORK CITY

All seats $2.00

Tickets available at: The Folklore Center
                          110 MacDougal Street
GR 7 - 5987   New York City 12, New York

ABOVE
An advert for Bob's gig at the Folklore Center, November 1961. Joan referred to him in those days as an "urban hillbilly."

issues. I felt them in my bones," she wrote in her memoirs.
She broke up with Michael New around this time and when in
April 1962 she came back to New York for a gig and bumped
into Bob Dylan, she was instantly attracted to him. He played
her a song he had written, "With God on our Side," and she
was bowled over by it: "It's fair to say I fell under that spell
of his," she said. She was jealous when he asked if Mimi was
coming along to the party that night but managed to make a
joke of it. And she invited him to visit her on the West Coast
when he came over for the Monterey Festival. The advice of
the friend who told him that he should "start screwing Joan
Baez" must have been in the back of his mind.

Folk royalty

Bob's set at the 1962 Monterey Festival wasn't going down too
well until Joan walked out on stage to join him. She announced
to the crowd that this young man had something to say for
everyone who wanted a better world. They sang a duet of "With
God on our Side" and when they left the stage 20,000 people
were cheering. Bob came back to Joan's house afterward, she

BELOW
*Bob and Joan duetted
on "When the Ship
Comes In" at the 1968
March for Freedom
where Martin Luther
King, Jr. delivered his
"I Have a Dream"
speech. Black nationalist
Malcolm X later said
he didn't think any
white people should
have been involved.*

made stew, and they played music together. "I wanted to mother him and he seemed to want it and need it," she said. "I was falling in love." Back in New York, unbeknown to Joan, Bob was still seeing Suze Rotolo, but she was beginning to tire of his frequent infidelities. She was pictured with him on the cover of his 1963 album *The Freewheelin' Bob Dylan*, but by the time it came out their relationship was crumbling.

During the summer of 1963, Bob and Joan appeared together at the Newport Folk Festival, and the press stories read, "Baez, the reigning queen of folk music, has named Dylan the crown prince." They toured that fall and she played and sang his songs, introducing him to her legions of fans, generously telling them, "You may not know his name but you should." Backstage, she hand-washed his shirts, arranged his hair, and most of all they laughed together: "We were getting close, it was very sweet between us," she later recalled. After the tour Bob came back to stay with her in the Carmel Highlands. "I lived with her and I loved the place," he said. While he spent the days writing, she kept house and brought him snacks. She thought he was a genius, "the modern Shakespeare," and saved first drafts he had thrown in the trash. But still Bob flirted with her sister Mimi, which must have been dispiriting. And back in New York that winter he once again called Suze and they were briefly reunited.

RIGHT
The March on Washington, August 28, 1963, was attended by over 250,000 people.

THE PEACE QUEEN

In 1956, Joan heard Martin Luther King, Jr. speak about nonviolence and social equality and was so moved and inspired that she determined to work for the civil rights movement herself. On August 28, 1963, she dragged Bob to the March for Freedom from the Washington Monument to the Lincoln Memorial, but joked that she had to use a cattle prod to get him there because "it wasn't really his thing." At the end of the day she sang, "We Shall Overcome," a powerful anthem that became associated with her from then on. In 1964, she withheld 60 percent of her income tax from the government, the portion that would have been spent on armaments for the escalating situation in Vietnam. In the same year she set up The Institute for the Study of Non-Violence in Carmel, and throughout the rest of the 1960s she protested in support of men who resisted the draft, getting arrested twice in the process and spending almost a month in jail altogether. Her position in this and each subsequent campaign she has supported is clear—equality for all, opposition to war and the death penalty, and, more recently, saving the planet.

"ALL I CAN SAY IS POLITICS IS NOT MY THING"

BELOW
Bob recording the album Bringing It All Back Home in January 1965. Joan said that while he was writing it the previous summer, "he stood at the typewriter in the corner of his room, drinking red wine and smoking and tapping away relentlessly for hours."

Throughout 1964, Joan praised Bob at every concert she gave, and he dedicated his encores to her. He was beginning to feel uncomfortable with the strength of her political activism, though, particularly as a white man dabbling in the civil rights movement. "All I can say is politics is not my thing," he explained, but Joan urged him on and didn't see any warning signs. She felt they were closer than ever that summer, both recognizing the other's fragility and offering support. She was still insecure about her looks and wore a light sweater over her bikini at the pool to hide her breasts, which she felt were too small. He bought a Triumph 350 motorbike but was such a terrible driver that Joan usually drove it while he clung on behind. According to Joan, they began to talk playfully about the future, and even discussed what they would name their baby one day. And then one night on the phone, while he was on the East Coast and she on the West, she jokingly brought up the subject of marriage, just testing the ground, and when he didn't respond she said something offhand, like "Oh, you know, it'd never work out." From that point on, she felt things were never the same again—after that, "it was as though he was playing around with my soul."

The bitter end

By the end of 1964, the ground had shifted and Bob was becoming so famous in his own right that he didn't need Joan anymore. They did ten tour dates together that winter and Bob later admitted, "I knew it was over. She gets such a morgue audience . . . it was like playing in a funeral parlor." Joan recalled, "I asked him what made us different, and he said it was simple, that I thought I could change things,

and he knew no one could." His increasing cynicism bothered her, as did the fact that he now booked them separate but adjacent rooms on tour. Musically they were going in different directions as well, with him heading toward a rock feel in the album *Bringing It All Back Home*, which he made in January 1965. When she visited him on the East Coast in the spring, he alternately ignored her or

ABOVE
Sara Lowndes and Bob began their relationship in late 1964. According to Dylan biographer Robert Shelton, she seemed to be "wise beyond her years, knowledgeable about magic, folklore, and traditional wisdom."

was rude to her. On one occasion he was so awful that her sister Mimi grabbed his hair, yanked his head back, and screamed, "Don't you ever treat my sister that way again."

Bob's UK tour between the end of April and early June 1965 was being filmed by director Bob Pennebaker for a documentary that would come to be titled *Don't Look Back* when released in 1967. What Joan didn't know was that Bob had been introduced to Pennebaker by a girl called Sara Lowndes, a former model, who was already his new girlfriend. Ever-secretive, Bob had rented a room in the Chelsea Hotel so he could meet Sara in private. Several people on the tour knew of their budding relationship—but not Joan. She blithely flew to England only to be crushed when Bob told her she couldn't sing on stage with him. It would have been nice for him to introduce her to UK audiences the way she had done for him in the US, but he didn't feel the need to return any favors. By May 5, things were going so badly that Joan wrote to Mimi, "he has become so unbelievably unmanageable that I can't stand to be around him," adding that she was "incredibly battered by the whole thing." She left after Bob and a friend started joking about her breasts in front of her. A few weeks later she heard Bob had been admitted to hospital suffering from a stomach problem, so she flew back to London to visit

WOODSTOCK, AUGUST 15–18, 1969

It was the festival that defined a generation. Dairy farmer Max Yasgur offered his land in Bethel, New York, and the organizers told local authorities they expected a maximum of 50,000 people. However, as one big-name act after another agreed to play at the three-day event, it became clear they were seriously underestimating numbers. The night before, crowds cut through the perimeter fence and folk flooded in, causing traffic gridlock for miles around. Those who got there (estimated at half a million) weren't disappointed by the show, given that Joan Baez, Janis Joplin, the Grateful Dead, The Who, and Jimi Hendrix were among the attractions. The Band, who backed Bob Dylan from 1965 to 1974, also played, but he didn't appear despite living locally; he was said to be grumpy about all the hippies turning up on his doorstep. Woodstock was a remarkably peaceful event despite bad weather and a lack of toilets. Two people died (one of a heroin overdose and the other run over by a tractor) and two babies were born (one in a car stuck in traffic and the other in a helicopter being airlifted to hospital). It was all captured in a 1970 movie and mythologized as the event that summed up the hippie values of peace and love.

him. At the door of his room she met Sara Lowndes: "And that's how I found out there was a Sara," she wrote in her memoirs.

Bob went on to marry Sara in Long Island in November 1965, but his parents, his brother David, and most of his friends knew nothing about it. They weren't even told when his son Jesse Byron Dylan was born in January 1966, the news only emerging after a journalist broke the story the following month. Bob and Sara's marriage produced four children and lasted twelve years but is said to have ended in 1977 after Sara came down to breakfast to find another of his lovers sitting at the table. Bob married again, to one of his backing singers, Carolyn Dennis, but he kept this union secret for fifteen years by installing her in a house in

an LA suburb where he came and went without notice. He was able to manage his overlapping relationships because of the length of time he spent on the road, averaging a hundred shows a year. "I'm just not the kind of person who seems to be able to settle down," he told a journalist in 2009.

It took Joan a while to recover from Bob's rejection, and especially the way he did it, which she called "the most demoralizing experience in my life." She said she "never understood how he could suddenly change, as if everything he had done before had never really happened." Maybe the truth is simpler: perhaps he just used her all along. "I rode on Joan, man," he admitted to a journalist. "You know? I'm not proud of it." He later admitted that the craziness of the whole period screwed him up. There are clues in the lyrics of some of the half a dozen songs he wrote while with Joan, including, "Love is Just a Four Letter Word." On the other hand, Joan didn't hold a grudge, with her 1975 song "Diamonds &

"I WAS CRAZY ABOUT HIM. WE WERE AN ITEM AND WE WERE HAVING A WONDERFUL TIME"

Rust" an affectionate if bittersweet look back at their affair. Bob said he was honored by it and invited her to play on his "Rolling Thunder Revue" tour in late 1975/early 1976. She even put him up for a few weeks after his marriage to Sara ended. And both Bob and Joan were magnanimous about each other in a 2009 documentary entitled *How Sweet the Sound*. He praises "Joanie" for her commitment to social causes and she admits just how much she used to love him: "I was crazy about him. We were an item and we were having a wonderful time."

ABOVE
Joan in 2007. She wrote in her autobiography, "I am made to live alone."

"WE WERE BOUND TOGETHER, TWO PEOPLE WHO NEEDED EACH OTHER"

SONNY
&
CHER

ROCK 'N' ROLL

**SALVATORE PHILLIP
"SONNY" BONO**

Born: February 16, 1935
Detroit, Michigan

Died: January 5, 1998
Stateline, Nevada

CHERILYN SARKISIAN

Born: May 20, 1946
El Centro, California

Married: March 4, 1969
Los Angeles, California

Sonny and Cher both grew up desperate to be famous and they found in each other a route to stardom as well as a romantic partner. She had the big voice and he managed the business side. What could possibly go wrong?

Cher was just sixteen and had recently run away from home when she met Sonny while hanging out with some friends in an LA coffee shop. "Too bad he's so short," she thought—at five foot six inches, he was two-and-a-half inches shorter than her—but then she listened to his conversation and realized first of all that he was very funny and, second, that he seemed to know a lot of influential people in the music business. They arranged a double date but it was Cher's friend Sonny was interested in, having formed the opinion that Cher was arrogant. She wasn't, but she did cover her insecurities with a sharp tongue and snappy comebacks that often gave that impression. It wasn't long before she fell for the very charming Sonny and when her roommate left and she found herself homeless, she somehow persuaded him to let her move in to his home and become his cook and cleaner. Soon she was transcending normal employer–employee relations, borrowing his Fruit of the Loom underpants and slipping into his bed if she had a nightmare (he consented so long as she didn't waken him). Sonny found she was very gullible and enjoyed teasing her—among other jokes, he persuaded her that he was a descendant of Napoleon Bonaparte and his father had shortened the family name to Bono. He even convinced her that the presidents' heads on Mount Rushmore were natural phenomena.

OPPOSITE
Coming together: Sonny wore boots with built-up heels to reach Cher's height, and she sang in his register because he didn't have much of a vocal range.

BELOW
Good Times (1967) is a movie about Sonny and Cher making a movie while trying to retain their integrity.

LOOK WHO'S MAKING THE MOVIE SCENE!

COLUMBIA PICTURES presents

Sonny & Cher in "Good Times"

GEORGE SANDERS and NORMAN ALDEN

Screenplay by TONY BARRETT · Story by NICHOLAS HYAMS · Music Composed and Conducted by SONNY BONO · Executive Producer STEVE BRODY
Produced by LINDSLEY PARSONS · Directed by WILLIAM FRIEDKIN · A MOTION PICTURE INTERNATIONAL PRODUCTION
Color by DeLuxe® C

"IT WASN'T A FIERY, SEXY THING WITH US"

As she wandered around his apartment cleaning, Cher used to sing to herself and Sonny's ears pricked up at the sound of her huge, booming contralto voice. He worked in the music business, promoting records to radio DJs and writing his own (so far unsuccessful) songs. Cher wanted to be an actress and was taking acting classes but Sonny persuaded her to come to producer Phil Spector's studio with him. When he heard her voice, Spector gave her work as a backing singer on a number of tracks, including "Da Doo Ron Ron" by The Crystals and "You've Lost That Lovin' Feeling" by The Righteous Brothers. It was during this period that her relationship with Sonny was finally consummated. "It wasn't a fiery, sexy thing with us," she said, "but rather paternal, like we were bound together, two people who needed each other almost for protection."

Sonny had total belief in Cher's talents and turned all his efforts to writing and producing songs he hoped would launch her singing career. The first ones they recorded didn't take off, but in 1965 they released their first album and it was time to tour, to reach out to audiences. Cher was so terrified of performing live that she sometimes fainted before shows, so they decided to work as a duo, despite the fact he couldn't sing; she could hide her stage fright by singing directly to him and pretending the audience wasn't there. And so they became Sonny and Cher.

A long uphill climb

Both Sonny and Cher came from impoverished backgrounds that instilled in them a hunger for fame and fortune. He was born in Detroit, the third son in an Italian family, at a time when industry was still struggling to emerge from the Great Depression. When Sonny was seven, his father moved to California to look for work and the family went out to join him after he got established as a truck driver. His parents wanted him to go into higher education, but he dropped out of school after eleventh grade to work as a delivery boy and try to make his way in the music business. He'd grown up listening to his dad playing banjo and accordion at home, and while at school he and a friend entertained classmates by playing the

hits of the day on piano, conga drum, and ukulele. Sonny
taught himself to play by listening to the radio and working
out the chords, and he wrote his first song, "Ecstasy," in 1952,
but it failed to break into the charts. For a while he wrote songs
for Crystal Records, owned by singer Frankie Laine, before
moving to an independent label called Specialty Records, which
had a roster of black artists including Little Richard and Sam
Cooke. Sonny wrote some B-sides for them and produced Sam
Cooke's "I'll Come Running Back to You," but was fired after
they found out he was moonlighting for other artists. He'd got
married in 1954 to a girl called Donna Rankin, and they had
a baby daughter called Christine, but the marriage broke up
after his sacking from Specialty when they were thrown out
of their home, which he had rented from the boss. In 1961,
when Sonny met Cher, he was working for an LA company
called Record Merchandising. It wasn't a great job, but he was
a big talker and right away she saw him as someone who knew
his way around.

 Cher's mother had always wanted to be a star. She sang
in bars and on local radio, and got small roles
in movies, but she had lousy taste in men.
By 1985, she had been married eight times
altogether, three of them to Cher's father,
John Sarkisian, a heavy drinker and gambler
who spent time in jail and had virtually
no relationship with his daughter. When
Cher was young, they were very poor.
"I remember going to school with rubber
bands around my shoes to keep the soles
on," she says. When she was fourteen, her
mother married a bank manager and
the family fortunes looked up.
Cher was sent to a private
school in Encino—her
fifteenth school or
thereabouts—where she
learned to hone her
sharp, defensive ripostes
to combat the hostility
of the other girls. But

BELOW
*"Cher wanted to be an
entertainer more than
I've seen anybody want
to be an entertainer in
my life," Sonny said, and
his own ambition easily
matched hers.*

CHER'S STYLE

With her long, straight black hair and striking features, Cher's looks drew attention, and she developed a clothes style of her own from the start. She didn't like the short skirts of the '60s as they exposed her bow legs, so she popularized pants that flared out from the knees, known as bell bottoms, which she wore with beaded tops inspired by her Cherokee ancestry or with short tank tops that left a bare midriff (she was the first woman to expose her navel on TV), as well as bandanas round her head. During the 1970s she discovered designer Bob Mackie and began to favor his skin-tight, cutaway, sequinned dresses. As a solo performer in the '80s and '90s, her costumes became ever-more excessive and were worn with tall, feathered headdresses or huge colored wigs. She frequently appears on the Best-Dressed List, although sometimes also on the Worst-Dressed, and in 1999 was given an award by the Council of Fashion Designers of America for her influence on fashion. There have been imitators since, but Cher was the original style queen who blended ethnicity with bling, for whom no extra string of beads would ever be considered de trop.

no matter how hard she worked she never did well at school, only finding out decades later that she was dyslexic. At sixteen, she left home and started to take acting classes. "I just thought, well, I'll be famous," she later said. "That was my goal."

Sonny Bono seemed like a good bet. They had the same dreams and he knew people who could help take them there. She'd had relationships before, but she knew early on that this was the real thing. Both she and Sonny had the same persistent streak, and this kept them trying song after song in an attempt to break through. They recorded their first unsuccessful single, "Ringo, I Love You," at Phil Spector's suggestion, but it wasn't until 1964 that Cher had her first hit with "Baby Don't Go," written by Sonny. The following summer, "I Got You, Babe," also written by Sonny, spoke of their feelings for each other. It zoomed up to number one in the US charts, appealing to a generation of hippies who loved the song's sentiments and also copied Sonny and Cher's

costumes of flower-patterned, bell-bottomed pants, fake-fur tank tops, and beads. Suddenly they had what they'd been dreaming of— they were famous, and they liked the feeling.

From squares to TV stars

Reporters soon wanted to know if Sonny and Cher were married. They didn't want the media circus a wedding would entail so claimed they had wed in Tijuana, Mexico, on October 27, 1964. In fact, they had been in Tijuana that day but had merely exchanged $12 silver rings in their hotel bathroom (it would be 1969 before they legally married, after the birth of their daughter). They went on tour and, in a preplanned PR stunt, were thrown out of London's smart Hilton Hotel because their hippy clothes were deemed unsuitable. More hits followed—"Laugh at Me" and "Bang Bang (My Baby Shot Me Down)"—with Cher putting her heart and soul into every song. She wasn't so comfortable when Sonny got them making a movie, *Good Times,* because she didn't like the script and felt awkward in front of the cameras, but she did enjoy TV appearances on shows such as *Hullaballoo.* "We were with each other twenty-four hours a day," she told *Ladies' Home Journal,* "and we fought less than any other couple I have ever known." And both loved the money their fame brought. In 1967, they purchased a thirty-one-room mansion in LA's exclusive Holmby Hills area and decorated it in colorful, excessive style. She drove an Excalibur car while he had an Aston Martin and several motorcycles. Anything they wanted, they could afford.

And then they made a mistake: in early 1968 they agreed to make an antidrugs film for distribution in schools, and Sonny spoke out against the legalization of abortion. Such views lost them the support of their fan base. "Hippies thought we were square; squares thought we were hippies. And Sonny and Cher were down the toilet," Cher explained. For the next three years, none of their records would make the charts. Sonny sank all their money into developing a movie called *Chastity,* about a damaged young woman drifting in and out of relationships,

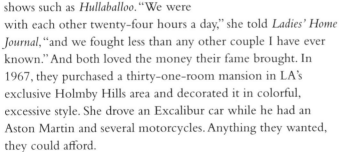

"HIPPIES THOUGHT WE WERE SQUARE; SQUARES THOUGHT WE WERE HIPPIES"

ABOVE
With their baby, Chastity Sun Bono, in August 1970. Chastity made many guest appearances on The Sonny & Cher Comedy Hour, which ran from 1971 to 1974.

OPPOSITE
Cher in a Bob Mackie dress—if it was glittery, skin-tight, cutaway, and virtually transparent, then she loved it.

ABOVE
The Sonny & Cher
Comedy Hour. *Guest
comedian Freeman King
said, "There was always
a sadness about Cher . . .
She seemed like a lonely
person to me and she
and Sonny didn't
socialize with anybody
on the show."*

and he even remortgaged the house. Cher didn't want to do
it but, she said, "You do not disagree with Sonny." On set they
argued over dialogue, and Cher had to hide her advancing
pregnancy. The child, born in March 1969, was named Chastity,
after the movie. But when it was released, *Chastity* tanked:
"Completely banal," said the *New York Times*.

At the end of 1970, Sonny finally confessed to Cher that
they were broke and would have to move out of their dream
home. She refused to budge and instead they brainstormed a
new double act in which he chatted with the audience and she
criticized him with deadpan delivery—his height, his Italian
ancestry, his off-key singing—everything was fair game. She
changed her hippie outfits for glitzy long dresses and they
took their act on the nightclub circuit, slogging it out in small
venues to pay $190,000 back taxes. After a successful stint on
Merv Griffin's TV show, they were commissioned to make
their own *Sonny & Cher Comedy Hour* and soon the show
was attracting 25 million viewers per episode—35% of the
viewing public. In September 1971, the song "Gypsies, Tramps
& Thieves" saw Cher storming back up to the number one slot.
But while their self-reinvention had put them back on top, the
relationship behind the celebrity couple was not doing so well.

Cher Enterprises

Sonny and Cher didn't have a social life. She later claimed that he was a "dictator" who decided everything, from the movies they watched and the music they listened to through to the people they saw. It was a "stultifying existence" that she went along with because she believed she would never have gotten anywhere without him. In 1972 she was exhausted and asked if they could have a vacation in Europe, but Sonny said they were too busy. It was the final straw. Without warning, she told him she was leaving. "Something had been building in her for years, I guess," he said later, still puzzled. He told her that America would hate her if word got out because of the popularity of their show, so they agreed to keep their separation private. She didn't have any money of her own and continued living in the Holmby Hills house and working on the show while dating a saxophone player from their backing band. When the couple presented the Oscars in February 1973, they were all smiles for the cameras but completely ignored each other backstage.

The situation couldn't last forever and in September 1973, Cher met music business executive David Geffen, who fell in love with her. As they talked, he realized she knew nothing about the business side of "Sonny and Cher" and decided to help her claim her fair share of the assets. Sonny filed for legal separation in February 1974, citing "irreconcilable differences," then at the end of the month he was stunned when she sued him for divorce on grounds of "involuntary servitude," claiming that he had "unlawfully dominated and controlled [her] business interests and career" in breach of her rights under the 13th Amendment. Sonny, reeling from the tactic, told reporters, "Cher was never an involuntary anything. I'm not prepared to be cast in the role of the villain." They talked, and she agreed to back down if he gave her half of everything—he refused.

When he investigated their affairs, Geffen found that Cher was an employee of a company called Cher Enterprises, 95 percent of which was owned by Sonny and the other 5 percent by their lawyer. She was entitled to just three weeks' vacation a year and couldn't work for any other

BELOW
Sonny with David Geffen, whom she was with for two years. She said, "I never felt that I left Sonny for another man. I left him for a woman. Me."

HUSBAND-&-WIFE BANDS

One of the problems with being married to a rock star is that they're in the studio or on tour the whole time, but at least if you are in the band you can keep each other company and fend off the groupies. Rock history is full of husband-and-wife teams—Sonny and Cher, Ike and Tina Turner, June Carter and Johnny Cash, Womack and Womack—but the pressures of working together day in, day out, take their toll, and it requires an exceptionally strong couple to survive. ABBA was formed when two married couples—Benni Andersson and Anni-Frid Lyngstad, Agnetha Fältskog and Björn Ulvaeus—got together, and their music dominated the charts worldwide from 1975 to 1982. However, when both marriages fell apart, so did the band. During the making of the best-selling Fleetwood Mac album *Rumours* in 1976, three long-term band relationships bit the dust: Stevie Nicks and Lindsey Buckingham, who'd known each other since school days, split acrimoniously; Christine McVie left John, her husband of eight years; and Mick Fleetwood had an affair with Stevie Nicks that led to the end of his marriage with Jenny Boyd, with whom he had two daughters.

company until 1977—and even then Sonny would have a claim on her future earnings. She had signed the paperwork without reading it because she had no interest in business. Sonny claimed the company had simply been a vehicle to stop them running up the kind of debts they had accrued in the late '60s. The legal battles began and were played out both in and out of court. Neither wanted to give up the Holmby Hills mansion, but in July 1974, Cher and Geffen took possession of it with armed security guards. She won custody of Chastity with Sonny getting visitation rights at weekends. Finally, their business affairs were separated. Sonny never blamed Cher for the legal battles but he hated Geffen with a passion.

The best of friends

After the split, Sonny presented a TV show on his own but it bombed. He acted in some TV dramas and a few movies, then in 1988 he found a brand-new direction in life when he was voted Mayor of Palm Springs. In 1994, he was elected to the House of Representatives, where one of his causes involved the extension of copyright to protect artists' rights. He married twice more after his divorce from Cher and had two more children.

ABOVE
*Cher with Olympia
Dukakis in* Moonstruck
*(1987). During her
career, Cher has won
a Best Actress Oscar,
three Golden Globes, an
Emmy, and a Grammy.
"I think that's maybe
my best quality: I just
don't stop," she said
in 2010.*

Cher's relationship with Geffen didn't last, but she married singer/songwriter Greg Allman three days after her divorce from Sonny came through, only to try to dissolve the marriage just nine days later, realizing she had underestimated his dependence on drugs. There were a number of separations and reconciliations, and they had a child together, Elijah Blue, but in the end she left because "I loved him but I didn't really want Elijah around him alone." A string of younger lovers followed, but she has never remarried. Her career soared onward and upward, both as actress and singer. She starred in a number of successful movies and won the Best Actress Oscar in 1988 for her role in the romantic comedy *Moonstruck.* Her music reached new heights with the 1989 platinum album *Heart of Stone,* and the chart-topping singles "If I Could Turn Back Time" (1989) and "Believe" (1998), among many others, in a career that has seen her have a number one record in each of five decades.

> "NO MATTER HOW LONG I LIVE OR WHO I MEET IN MY LIFE, SONNY WAS THE MOST UNFORGETTABLE CHARACTER"

Against the odds, she and Sonny stayed friends and sometimes called each other to ask advice or simply to chat. She was devastated when the news reached her in January 1998 that he had died after a skiing accident. She gave a tearful eulogy at his funeral, at which she said, "No matter how long I live or who I meet in my life, he was the most unforgettable character." They'd been everything to each other—spouse, best friend, parent, sibling, and costar—and the combination was simply too much to sustain. But right to the end they never stopped loving each other.

OPPOSITE
*Sonny being sworn
in to the House of
Representatives in 1994,
with Speaker of the
House Newt Gingrich.
Sonny is the only
member of Congress
ever to have had a
number one hit single.*

"WITH VELVET BROWN EYES
AND DARK CHESTNUT HAIR,
HE WAS THE BEST-LOOKING
MAN I'D EVER SEEN"

GEORGE HARRISON
&
PATTIE BOYD

ROCK 'N' ROLL

GEORGE HARRISON

Born: February 25, 1943
Liverpool, UK

Died: November 29, 2001
Beverly Hills, California

**PATRICIA ANNE
"PATTIE" BOYD**

Born: March 17, 1944
Taunton, UK

★

Married: January 21, 1966
Epsom, UK

When George met Pattie in January 1964, Beatlemania was already in full swing, so as well as the normal pressures faced by any young couple they had to cope with the intense, surreal aspects of life under the media spotlight and the almost constant pursuit of the Fab Four by hordes of screaming fans.

While George's mother was pregnant with him, she regularly tuned in to Radio India, hoping that the exotic music they played, with sitars and tablas, would make him a peaceful child. It certainly made him a musical child: while he was still at elementary school he persuaded his mom to buy him a second-hand guitar for three pounds, and he and his brother formed their own skiffle group called The Rebels. When he heard Elvis Presley's "Heartbreak Hotel" on pirate radio station Radio Luxembourg, "the tune lodged itself permanently in the back of my brain," as he later wrote in his memoirs. In 1954 he started his high-school education at the Liverpool Institute and made friends with Paul McCartney, another kid on the bus who shared his love of rock 'n' roll. Then in July 1957, Paul met John Lennon, who invited him to join his band, The Quarrymen. The following year Paul brought George to meet them but, although impressed with his playing, John thought George was too young at the age of fifteen to be allowed to join. He began stepping in as a substitute when another guitar player let them down and later replaced founder member Eric Griffiths in the band that was renamed The Beatles.

George's bus conductor father didn't consider being a musician a steady career, so when George left school his dad persuaded him to start work as an apprentice electrician, giving him a set of screwdrivers as a Christmas present. But in August 1960, when The Beatles got a gig at a club in Hamburg, George didn't think twice about going. He was only seventeen and legally too young

OPPOSITE
At their wedding, January 21, 1966. "It was not the wedding I had dreamed of," said Pattie. "I would have loved to be married in a church but . . . it had to be secret—if the press found out it would be chaos."

BELOW
George with John Lennon and Stuart Sutcliffe in The Quarrymen, a skiffle band John had formed in 1956.

to work in Germany, but they managed to sneak him through immigration and their shows at the Indra and the Kaiserkeller over the next hundred days quickly became sellouts. The experience gave the band the chance to develop their musical skills and stage presence. Back in Liverpool in February 1961, they played the legendary Cavern Club and developed an instant following. They came to the attention of local businessman Brian Epstein when a fan came into his store asking for a copy of one of their songs. Brian got them a contract with record company EMI and their first single, "Love Me Do," made it to number 17 in the charts in late 1962, before the album *Please Please Me* became the UK's top seller for thirty weeks the following year. George was just twenty years old and dazzled by the adulation. He idolized John Lennon, and tagged along with the rest of the boys when they went out partying and meeting girls. Although he was the quiet one on stage, and shy off stage, he liked girls and didn't have any trouble picking them up.

In January 1964, the band were filming a sequence for their movie *A Hard Day's Night* on a train between London and Cornwall. One of the extras was a model called Pattie Boyd and George's head was completely turned by her big cornflower-blue eyes, her waist-length blonde hair, and her bubbly, chatty personality. He contrived to sit next to her at

BELOW
The Fab Four with their moptop hairstyles. George was the first to have his hair cut this way, inspired by Jürgen Vollmer, a photographer he met in Hamburg.

lunch and asked, "Will you marry me?" She giggled, unsure how to respond. "Well," he continued, "if you won't marry me, will you have dinner with me tonight?" He was crestfallen when she told him she couldn't because she already had a boyfriend. It wasn't a response he was used to in those days as The Beatles' popularity soared to stratospheric levels.

The crazy side of fame

Pattie's childhood was shaped by her parents' marriage breakup and frequent moving around. At the age of four the family traveled out to Kenya to stay with her wealthy grandparents, where she was largely cared for by nannies while her parents went their separate ways. She attended convent school in Nairobi then was sent to boarding school in Nakuru at the age of eight, an experience that left her feeling "unloved, unwanted, unimportant." In December 1953, she was uprooted again and sent back to England where her mother introduced her to a new stepfather, a bully who was unpopular with Pattie and her three younger siblings. The family had only just been reunited when Pattie was sent away to yet another boarding school. She heard nothing from her real father except for an occasional Christmas card, and when her stepfather ran off with a neighbor, she felt it must be her fault in some way.

On leaving school, Pattie got a job in an Elizabeth Arden salon in London and shared a tiny apartment with a school friend. A client at the salon encouraged her to try modeling for *Honey* magazine, and she was soon taken on by a modeling agency and began to get regular work for fashion magazines. Her first serious boyfriend, the photographer Eric Swayne, arrived on the scene around this time and helped introduce her to editors who could give her work. He wanted her to be

"IF YOU WON'T MARRY ME, WILL YOU HAVE DINNER WITH ME TONIGHT?"

ABOVE
During the Hard Day's Night *shoot, the boys had their hair styled by schoolgirls. Pattie is the one on the far left who is working on George.*

THE BEATLE-MAKER

Brian Epstein was working for his parents' furniture stores in Liverpool when he signed up The Beatles, even though he had no experience of managing music business contracts. He arranged one deal that naively gave 51 percent of the copyright in Lennon/McCartney compositions to a company called Northern Songs as a result of which the pair lost control of all publishing rights after the company was sold. But they never blamed Brian. He was the "fifth Beatle," according to Paul McCartney, and they always acknowledged their debt to him. Not only did he get them a record deal and mold their image (persuading them to drop leather jackets and jeans in favor of suits and ties), but he also brought a touch of class, teaching them the wine they should order in upscale restaurants and which knives and forks to use. In an era when homosexuality was still illegal in Britain, they knew Brian was gay but were fiercely protective of him. They also knew he was dependent on pills, using "uppers" to stay up late, then "downers" to get to sleep. He was due to join The Beatles in Wales in 1967 when he died suddenly of a lethal combination of pills and alcohol, believed to be accidental.

RIGHT
George with the ultra-suave, sophisticated Brian Epstein.

"his model," the way Jean Shrimpton was for David Bailey, and he became her first lover as well. Eric was ambitious, but Pattie wasn't comfortable with the absurdities of that world. In November 1963, she felt shy when asked to make a commercial in which she ate potato chips and lisped how much she loved them, and when, soon afterward, her agent told her she'd got a part as a schoolgirl in a Beatles movie, she was simply terrified. But she needn't have worried as, once she arrived on set, she found herself beginning to relax in the atmosphere of easy camaraderie that existed among the Liverpool lads.

Every girl had her own favorite Beatle and after meeting them, Pattie's was definitely George. "With velvet brown eyes and dark chestnut hair, [he] was the best-looking man I'd ever seen," she wrote in her autobiography. When he asked her out she was flustered. She had been dating Eric for nine months and they were semiengaged, although her feelings were fading. Still, it didn't seem right to accept a date with another man. "You're crazy!" her roommate screamed on hearing she had turned down George Harrison. But another day's filming was scheduled for March 12 and, before that,

Pattie broke up with Eric so was able to accept George's dinner invitation with a clear conscience the second time he asked.

Bizarrely, Brian Epstein accompanied them on their first date, at London's Garrick Club. Perhaps his presence helped to break the ice, as both George and Pattie were so shy. They began seeing each other on a regular basis and before long she was being introduced to life in The Beatles' entourage when on a trip to Dublin she had to be smuggled out of their hotel in a laundry basket to escape the pursuing journalists. Pattie soon realized the downsides of dating a famous musician, from being left alone as the band were away on tour much of the time to receiving hate mail from jealous fans. She moved into George's house, Kinfauns, about forty-five minutes outside London, but there were always fans at the gate who broke into the grounds and stole things from the house given half a chance. The upside of the relationship was that she and George were deeply in love. "He was so beautiful and so funny," Pattie later wrote, and it was obvious to all that he was utterly devoted to her. He told her that he wrote "Something (in the Way She Moves)" specifically about her, a number that Frank Sinatra called "the world's greatest love song."

Such was the influence of their manager that when George proposed to Pattie, he said, "Let's get married. I'll speak to Brian." Brian gave his permission and organized the event: a registry

BELOW
Pattie and George loved going out to restaurants, parties, clubs, and discos, but were equally happy in the projection room at home watching episodes of Rowan & Martin's Laugh-In.

office service in Epsom, with Paul McCartney as best man, followed by a press conference at which journalists deluged Pattie with questions about everything from their first date to when they planned to start a family. She blurted out that they wanted three children but not straightaway; there was still plenty of time.

The search for meaning

George and Pattie were both very spiritual people, and she accompanied him in the early stages of his spiritual awakening. They both became vegetarian after reading a book about veal farming, and both enjoyed relaxing with a marijuana joint after Bob Dylan introduced them to the drug. Then at a dinner party in April 1965, someone spiked their coffee with LSD, an experience that for George was very profound. "I fell in love, not with anything or anybody in particular," he said, "but with everything." He met Indian musician Ravi Shankar, who taught him how to play the sitar, sitting cross-legged and holding the bowl against his foot. Ravi gave George a copy of a book called *Autobiography of a Yogi*, of which George later recalled, "The moment I looked at that picture of Yogananda on the front of the book, his eyes went right through me." Pattie took a meditation course and raved about it to George, and soon they began taking trips to India to learn meditation techniques from another Indian mystic, Maharishi Mahesh Yogi, taking the other Beatles along with them in 1968. Pattie has since written, "the experience seemed to have answered some of the nagging questions [George] had about his life but it had taken some of the lightness out of his soul." On their return he became obsessed with meditation as he strove for enlightenment, and Pattie was alarmed when he claimed to see himself as Krishna, "the dark one," a spiritual being who is constantly surrounded by women.

Soon after the India trip in 1968, George had a fling with French model Charlotte Martin, an ex-girlfriend of Eric Clapton, the blues guitarist with whom he sometimes wrote and recorded. Pattie was shocked and felt "miserable and unloved."

> "I FELL IN LOVE, NOT WITH ANYTHING OR ANYBODY IN PARTICULAR," HE SAID, "BUT WITH EVERYTHING"

John and George with Maharishi Mahesh Yogi. He was sometimes known as the Giggling Guru because he laughed so much during interviews.

Around the same time, John Lennon split from his wife Cynthia and hooked up with Japanese artist Yoko Ono, while Paul McCartney split with his long-term girlfriend, Jane Asher, and got together with American photographer Linda Eastman. Gradually, tensions in the band began to simmer. George was unhappy that his songwriting was not taken as seriously as that of Lennon and McCartney; he'd been writing songs since 1963 but only ever managed to get two or three onto each album. Then, while filming *Let It Be* (1970), the peace-loving George actually came to blows with Paul, and it was clear the band didn't have long to go.

In the midst of all this, Pattie was introduced to Eric Clapton at a party and although she found him "shy and reticent," he took an immediate shine to her. He wrote to her confessing his feelings and told her he would turn to heroin if she didn't leave George for him. Although attracted to him, she turned him down. Eric then wrote the iconic ballad "Layla" about a man who falls in love with an unavailable woman. It was clearly about Pattie and she was very moved by it, but when Eric confessed his feelings to George, the soon-to-be ex-Beatle asked her to choose between them. She chose to stay with George.

The Beatles broke up in December 1970, amid a flurry of lawsuits—a traumatic time for George. He had bought a huge mansion with twenty-five bedrooms set in its own grounds, and he and Pattie set about restoring it. Pattie wasn't happy

THE STORIES BEHIND BEATLES SONGS

The song "Sexy Sadie," originally called "Maharishi," was inspired by John Lennon's disillusionment with the Indian guru after actress Mia Farrow accused him of making a move on her. George didn't believe this allegation and only let the song be released once the original title had been changed. Paul McCartney wrote "Lovely Rita" after being given a parking ticket by a warden called Meta Davis outside Abbey Road Studios. The Lennon/McCartney song "I am the Walrus" refers to the Lewis Carroll poem "The Walrus and the Carpenter," but the phrase "semolina pilchard" refers to Detective Sergeant Pilcher, famous for leading drugs raids on celebrities, including John and Yoko. "Hey Jude" was written by Paul McCartney to comfort John's son Julian Lennon during his parents' divorce. And "Lucy in the Sky with Diamonds" is said to have been inspired by a drawing Julian made at kindergarten, although everyone assumed it referred to LSD. The Beatles' songs are peppered with drug references, sexual double entendres, and little background noises like the "tit, tit, tit" on "Girl."

RIGHT
Persistence pays off—Eric Clapton with Pattie. They first met in 1970 but didn't marry until 1979.

with her life, though. George had persuaded her to give up modeling, so to fill her time she took up knitting, yoga, painting, and even had flying lessons. Cooking was her greatest passion, but when George invited three Hare Krishna families to move in with them, they took over the kitchen, making his favourite Indian dishes. With so many people in the house, Pattie and George were never alone. He was meditating for hours on end, he was writing and playing music, and he was still being unfaithful to Pattie. She tried to turn a blind eye, but it hurt terribly when the woman in question was a friend of hers. And when he slept with Ringo Starr's wife Maureen, Pattie found it unbearable. On July 3, 1973, she flew to California to stay with her sister Jennie. While she was there, Eric Clapton invited her to join him on tour. How could Pattie refuse the man who had written "Layla" just for her?

Moving on

George accepted Pattie and Eric's relationship with seemingly yogic detachment. When he next met an apologetic Clapton, he shrugged and said, "Well, I suppose I'd better divorce her." In December 1977 he married Olivia

Arias, who worked for his record label in California. Two years later at Pattie and Eric's wedding, George introduced himself as "the husband-in-law," and from then on Pattie knew he would always be there for her.

According to Pattie, marriage to Eric was "like hitching a ride on a shooting star." He had kicked a heroin habit only to replace it with alcohol dependency. He wrote another beautiful song about Pattie—"Wonderful Tonight"—but he couldn't be faithful. Still, they started IVF treatments in an attempt to have a baby together. Pattie was past forty and desperate for a child, so it felt like a real kick in the teeth when Eric told her that an Italian girl called Lori was pregnant by him. She left him and went back to England. By this time George and Olivia had a son, Dhani, and she could only feel happy for them, though it seems she often wondered if things could have turned out differently. In her autobiography, she describes Eric as a "play mate" while George was her "soul mate."

ABOVE
George with Olivia Harrison. Olivia said that they "seemed like partners from the very beginning."

George's last two decades were rich but not without their challenges. He achieved brilliant success with his movie production company, HandMade Films, and was given an award by UNICEF for his humanitarian work. In a horrible echo of the murder of John Lennon, he was seriously injured in 1999 when a mentally ill man broke into his home and stabbed him repeatedly; his life was only saved by Olivia hitting the man over the head with a poker until he was unconscious. And then in 2001, at the age of fifty-eight, George died after a brief battle with lung cancer and a brain tumor. Pattie felt bereft for a long time—"I couldn't bear the thought of a world without George," she said—but she pulled herself together and created a new career exhibiting to great acclaim the photographs she had taken over the years she spent as wife and lover to two of the 20th-century's greatest rock stars.

"I PUT HIM THROUGH SUCH HELL. I MADE ALL THE TROUBLE. AND THROUGH ALL THIS HE REALLY ACTED PRACTICALLY LIKE A SAINT"

MICK JAGGER

&

MARIANNE FAITHFULL

ROCK 'N' ROLL

MICHAEL PHILIP JAGGER

Born: July 26, 1943
Dartford, UK

MARIANNE EVELYN FAITHFULL

Born: December 29, 1946
London, UK

★

Marianne was everything Mick wanted in a girl: well-spoken, with an aristocratic background; smart, with a lively, enquiring mind; beautiful, with big tits. She wasn't particularly drawn to him at first, describing the Stones as "yobbish schoolboys," but before long she succumbed to the glamor of their world.

When it comes to drugs, some people can take them or leave them while others get sucked in from the start. Having the gene for an addictive personality can tip the scales, and those with troubled backgrounds seem more susceptible to the lure of mind-altering chemicals. Marianne had the addictive gene, the unstable family, the desire to be hip—and she was lucky to get out alive after four years with Mick.

ABOVE
Marianne with John Dunbar in 1965. She spoke warmly of their marriage in her autobiography, saying, "I had a child with the right man."

Her mother, Eva von Sacher-Masoch, Baroness Erisso, was born in Vienna where she survived the war, hiding her Jewish roots, only to be raped by the Russian soldiers who liberated the city in 1945. Marianne's father, Glynn Faithfull, was a British spy—polite, charming, but madly eccentric. Eva saw in him an escape to gentility and safety, but instead he took the family to live in a commune in Oxfordshire. The marriage broke down when Marianne was six. She and her mother moved to Reading, where they lived on the breadline as, despite her title, the Baroness had no family money to fall back on and had to take a series of menial jobs to support them. They weren't Catholic but she sent Marianne as a charity boarder to St. Joseph's convent school, where the nuns were so strict that girls had to wear underslips in the bath so they didn't see their own naked bodies, which the sisters feared might lead them into temptation.

Marianne began to rebel in her teens, traveling to London to hang out in clubs, and eventually meeting her first lover, John Dunbar, when she was seventeen and he was twenty. In March 1964, a friend of John's took them to the party where she met the Stones, but it was their manager, Andrew Loog

OPPOSITE
Backstage at London's Royal Court Theatre in April 1967, after Marianne's first night in Chekhov's Three Sisters. She played the youngest sister—the sweet, innocent Irina.

Oldham, who made the strongest impression when he asked if she could sing, then offered her a record contract. "I saw an angel with big tits and signed her," he explained. A week later she was in the recording studio singing a song written by Mick Jagger and Keith Richards, "As Tears Go By." In the car to the station after the recording, Mick tried to make her sit on his knee but she refused. Next time they met, at a party for the *Ready Steady Go!* TV pop show, he poured champagne down her cleavage, but she simply walked away, unimpressed by his antics. In May 1965, she married John Dunbar, thinking marriage would help to ground her as her music career took off. The following November, when Marianne was still only eighteen, she had a son, Nicholas, but by then life in "Swinging London" had become far too exciting and her marriage was destined not to last. Before long she would be half of Britain's most notorious couple, and her world would be in a tailspin.

The aesthete & the aristo

Mick Jagger's family was as middle-class as they come—a father who was an athlete and a PE teacher and a hairdresser mother who originally hailed from Australia. At school in Dartford, Kent, Mike (as he was then known) was friends with a boy called Keith Richards, with whom he chatted about cowboys and guitars. Mike loved music: "I always sang as a child. I was one of those kids who just liked to sing."

He and Keith drifted apart when they went to different high schools, but a chance meeting at Dartford railway station when they were

BELOW
The Rolling Stones in 1965 (from left to right): Keith Richards, Brian Jones, Mick Jagger, Bill Wyman, and Charlie Watts. "We were young, good-looking and stupid," Mick said forty-five years later.

eighteen led to them getting together to play music. By this time Keith was at Sidcup Art School and Mick was studying business at the London School of Economics. They both loved rhythm-and-blues music, the sounds of Chuck Berry, Bo Diddley, and Little Richard, and joined a band formed by guitarist Brian Jones performing cover versions of R&B hits at a new blues club in London run by Alexis Korner. They acquired Andrew Loog Oldham as a manager, and gave their first performance as The Rolling Stones (the name came from a Muddy Waters track) at the Marquee Club on July 12, 1962. Oldham marketed them as an antidote to The Beatles. The Stones were the bad boys who inspired headlines such as "Would you let your daughter marry a Rolling Stone?" He also encouraged them to write their own music, and the Jagger/Richards songwriting partnership was formed, with Marianne's "As Tears Go By" one of their early compositions.

Mick loved being in a band: he loved the money, he loved performing, and he especially loved the girls who flocked backstage. With his huge lips and lithe, angular frame, he had an odd androgynous quality that was sexually attractive to both men and women, something he played on by wearing eye makeup and foppish velvet coats with lace shirts. In 1963, while still at college, he met his first serious girlfriend, the model Chrissie Shrimpton, whom he would date for three years. But the relationship was volatile due to his controlling behavior and constant infidelities. They got engaged and she moved into his apartment, but he was away on tour most of the time and she felt him drifting away. In December 1966, she took an overdose but was found in time and taken to hospital. She didn't know it, but Mick was already with Marianne Faithfull.

SLIDING DOWN THE HILL

On May 2, 1962, Brian Jones placed an ad in *Jazz News* inviting musicians to audition for a new R&B group at the Bricklayer's Arms pub in London. Pianist Ian Stewart came on board, then later Mick Jagger, who brought in Keith Richards, and the band Brian named The Rolling Stones was formed. Brian was the original leader, playing guitar, keyboards, and harmonica, and his use of traditional folk and jazz instruments shaped their musical direction. However, he soon felt alienated from the rest of the group as Mick and Keith started writing most of the music. He often traveled separately and stayed in different hotels on tour, and his overindulgence in alcohol and marijuana progressed into a cocaine and speed habit. In March 1967, when Anita Pallenberg, his girlfriend of two years, left him for Keith during a vacation in Tangiers, tensions increased further. Brian's second drugs arrest gave the band the ammunition they needed to get rid of him, because a conviction would make it difficult for them to get a US visa. On June 8, 1969, the other members visited him at his home and told Brian he was out. At midnight on July 2, he was found motionless in his swimming pool and was later pronounced dead.

ABOVE
"I wasn't trying to be rebellious in those days," Mick told a journalist in 1992. *"I was just being me ... the guy from suburbia who sings in a band, but someone older might have thought it was just the most awful racket, the most terrible thing, and where are we going if this is music?"*

Oldham had marketed Marianne as a virginal aristocratic type, all flowing blonde hair and floaty dresses. "As Tears Go By" made it to number nine in the UK charts in 1964, and over the next three years she made four singles and two albums, and undertook three tours. Her marriage fell apart as she hung out with Brian Jones and his girlfriend, the Italian model Anita Pallenberg, and started to smoke hash and take LSD with them. Mick kept pursuing her but in fact it was Keith Richards whom Marianne initially fell for: "I was in love with Keith, but very shyly," she says in her autobiography. She had one night of passion with him but next morning he told her she should go out with Mick. She realized that in the tangled web of band relationships, Keith was secretly in love with Anita.

Marianne went to see the band play in Bristol and at the end of the evening she invited Mick for a walk, where she quizzed him on Arthurian legend "to find out if he was serious." He answered all her questions correctly, and back at the hotel he carefully dried her wet boots—and then they made love. "He was affectionate, interesting, funny, and very attentive," she says. She had some misgivings about his reputation and the affair got off to a slow start, but in summer 1966, while she was playing the San Remo festival, she suddenly felt as though she wanted to see him. She phoned, he flew out to join her, and they hired a boat to cruise around the south of France, getting to know each other. When they got back to England, Marianne moved into the apartment only recently vacated by Chrissie. Mick was very generous, buying the shopaholic Marianne the clothes and jewelry she lusted after. He was a great stepfather to Nicholas, playing soccer and cricket with him, and he even bought a cottage for her mother. He introduced Marianne to a wide range of music and she introduced him to books, they vacationed together and they partook of a little acid, a little grass, a little alcohol. Everything should have been perfect—but Marianne always liked the drugs more than Mick did, and when he tried to make her stop, she simply went to Brian and Anita's dealer for her supplies.

"HE WAS AFFECTIONATE, INTERESTING, FUNNY, AND VERY ATTENTIVE"

The Redlands affair

In early February 1967, the *News of the World* ran an article purporting to quote Mick saying that he didn't take so much LSD now the fans had adopted it, but that he did use Benzedrine to stay awake. He instantly issued a libel action, perhaps a foolish move given that he was no drugs virgin. Soon afterward, on February 11, an anonymous caller told the police about a "drugs party" at Keith's house, Redlands. The police found eight men there along with Marianne, who was wrapped in a fur rug. They'd been out for a walk and her clothes had got muddy so she'd had a bath and there was nothing else to wear except the rug. During the ensuing search, the police found three tablets in Mick's pocket, which turned out to be travel-sickness pills Marianne had bought in Italy. The pills contained speed-like ingredients that were banned in the UK. Another guest had some heroin. Mick, Keith, and the other guest were charged with drugs offenses and when it came to trial, Mick was sentenced to three months in jail and a £200 fine. Marianne was distraught and begged him to allow her to confess the pills were hers, but he refused to "throw her to the wolves." In fact it was the editor of *The Times* newspaper who came to his rescue. Sir William Rees-Mogg wrote an editorial entitled "Who Breaks a Butterfly on a Wheel?" pointing out how ridiculous it was to be sentenced to jail for

BELOW
"Mick and I were like two children getting to know each other when this ferocious, full-blown story emerged out of nowhere," Marianne said of the Redlands affair. "My life had been stolen from me and sold to the gutter press."

possessing a tablet that the Pope could have taken legally in
Italy. Photographs of Mick in handcuffs caused a media storm
and he was released on bail after one night in jail and the
sentence was suspended—though he did have to drop his libel
action against the *News of the World*, despite strongly suspecting
the newspaper of being behind the anonymous call.

Mick shrugged off the furor and got on with making music,
but for Marianne it was devastating. She was identified in court
only as "Miss X," but when the police testimony talked of a
woman wrapped in a fur rug, everyone knew it referred to her.
On top of that, a completely falsified story went round that
the police had found her with a Mars bar in her vagina, which
Mick was licking. She described it as "a cop's idea of what
people do on acid," but the tale spread and became rock legend.
From being the virginal princess of Andrew Loog Oldham's
invention, overnight Marianne became the media archetype of
a drug-addled harlot. Her mother was so ashamed she stopped
going to work and Marianne began to get hate mail from the
public, calling her a slut and a bad mother. While Mick and
Keith's reputations were, if anything, enhanced, hers was in tatters.

Wild horses

Mick wanted to marry Marianne, but her divorce from John
wasn't yet finalized and in any case she felt quite overwhelmed
by the whole Stones lifestyle. She and Mick didn't get much
time on their own, and when they did she found it hard to get
him to open up. They moved to a new home and Marianne
enjoyed decorating it lavishly—"Six grand for a fuckin' light,"
Mick complained about a chandelier in the hallway. She got
pregnant and they were both delighted, deciding they would
call the baby Corrina. Marianne laid off the drugs and went to
rest in a cottage in the west of Ireland but she miscarried at five
months and was utterly distraught. To blot out the pain, she
began drifting deeper into drugs and when Mick tried to stop
her by withholding money, she simply had an affair with
a Spanish drug dealer.

Throughout the relationship, they were both unfaithful to
each other. Mick had a fling with Anita Pallenberg while making
the movie *Performance* in 1968, and then in July 1969 he hooked
up with the singer Marsha Hunt—and this was aside from all

OPPOSITE
*Marianne said that
Mick's infidelities
"brought out all
[her] feelings of
worthlessness."*

100

the groupies he could call on day and night. "Getting upset about a little fucking around was unhip and middle class," Marianne wrote in her autobiography, but she also admitted that she dealt with Mick's infidelities by retaliating in kind. "Oh, you fucked her? All right, I'll get you for that one. I'll see you and raise you one." And just when it seemed things could not get any worse, everyone was shocked and guilt-ridden when Brian Jones drowned in his swimming pool weeks after being asked to leave the band, a death that was probably accidental but undoubtedly connected to his excessive drug consumption.

ABOVE
Mick and Anita Pallenberg in Performance (1970)—it was rumored the sex scenes in the movie were "for real."

Six days after Brian's death, Mick and Marianne flew to Australia to film the movie *Ned Kelly*, in which she was to play his sister. Instead she took a massive overdose of 150 barbiturates and tried to jump out of their hotel room window, failing only because it was locked. Mick found her and took her to hospital

ALTAMONT

The concert on December 6, 1969 was billed as Woodstock West—a free festival featuring some of the great bands of the day, including the Rolling Stones. The venue was the Altamont Speedway, but this presented problems because the stage was at the bottom of a slope and was only three feet higher than the crowd. The band's security and that of their expensive equipment were potentially at risk, so the Stones' management arranged for members of the local Hell's Angels to stand in front of the stage. It was a loose arrangement for which they were paid $500 worth of beer. As the day progressed, the Angels got drunk and by the time the Stones took to the stage at sundown, there had been a number of fights between the Angels and the crowd, which numbered some 300,000. As Mick sang "Sympathy for the Devil," a fight erupted just in front of the stage and, despite the band's appeals for calm, 18-year-old Meredith Hunter was stabbed and killed after drawing a gun. Three others died: one drowned and two were killed in a hit-and-run accident. It was later described by *Rolling Stone magazine* as "rock and roll's all-time worst day."

where she lay in a coma for six days. "You've come back," he said as she opened her eyes. "You can't get rid of me that easily," she replied drowsily. "I thought I'd really lost you," Mick told her, to which she replied, "Wild horses wouldn't drag me away." It was the spark for a song he wrote entitled, "Wild Horses," one of many inspired by Marianne.

Mick paid for her to see a Swiss psychiatrist, but no one helped her come off drugs. The Stones toured America in the fall of 1969 and, in December that year, the band had another huge shock when a fight broke out and a member of the public was killed by Hell's Angels at a concert of theirs in Altamont, California. During this US tour, Mick was upset to read in the press that Marianne was having an affair with Mario Schifano, an ex-boyfriend of Anita Pallenberg. On his return to England he wooed her back, but the drug habit was so deeply entrenched that he couldn't reach her anymore. She left him again in early 1970, but still Mick tried to win her back until she changed her appearance drastically by cutting her hair and gaining fifty pounds in weight. After that, she later said, "He finally realized I wasn't on the market anymore."

RIGHT
Hell's Angels at Altamont—they hadn't wanted the role of policing the event.

Rock bottom

Mick moved Marsha Hunt into his London home, and Marianne had an affair with an Irish peer, Paddy Rossmore, but for both it was only the beginning of a long search for love. Mick married twice—to Nicaraguan Bianca De Macias and Texan model Jerry Hall—and he has since had a thirteen-year relationship with designer L'Wren Scott, which ended with her suicide in March 2014. He fathered seven children with four different mothers, and has become a multimillionaire through his work with the Stones, continuing to tour into his seventies. Marianne hit rock bottom after leaving Mick, losing custody of her son in 1970 and becoming a homeless heroin addict. Friends tried to help, but she was beyond reach until 1975, when she moved into a squat with Ben Brierly of punk band The Vibrators. Gradually she pulled her life back together and in 1979 released the critically acclaimed album *Broken English*. She married Brierly and remained with him till 1986; then in 1988 she married writer Giorgio Della Terza but they separated three years later; then she had a fifteen-year relationship with her manager, François Ravard, which ended in 2009—and all the while she was writing, performing music, and acting.

In her autobiography Marianne says she doesn't blame Mick for her terrible downward trajectory following the end of their affair: "I put him through such hell. I made all the trouble. And through all this he really acted practically like a saint." She was too fragile for the milieu of promiscuity, drugs, and rock 'n' roll Mick inhabited, while from the start he was a strong, determined character who could take the knocks and move on. He tried to do his best by Marianne, and he genuinely loved her, but he wouldn't let her underneath the carapace of his rock-star persona and expected her to be strong enough to cope with the pressures. "I was a victim of cool, of the tyranny of hip," she recalls, adding, "It almost killed me."

> ## "HE FINALLY REALIZED I WASN'T ON THE MARKET ANYMORE"

BELOW
Marianne was on the streets for two years and said of that time: "People looked after me, the meths drinkers, junkies. I learned that human beings are really all right."

"ALL YOU NEED IS LOVE"

JOHN LENNON & YOKO ONO

ROCK 'N' ROLL

JOHN WINSTON LENNON

Born: October 9, 1940
Liverpool, UK

Died: December 8, 1980
New York City

YOKO ONO

Born: February 18, 1933
Tokyo, Japan

Married: March 20, 1969
Gibraltar

Yoko was perhaps the most demonized woman of the 1970s because the press and fans believed her relationship with John had broken up The Beatles. But her only "crime" was to fall deeply and inexorably in love with a man who loved her just as much in return.

On her mother's side, Yoko was born into one of Japan's four wealthiest families, the Yasudas. Her father's relatives were noted artists, musicians, and academics, and her father could have been a classical pianist had he not chosen banking as a career. His work took him to the US, and he was living there when Yoko was born, not meeting her until she was two years old. She attended prestigious schools in Tokyo, but the family's eminence in society meant a lonely childhood without many playmates for Yoko, made more so with the approaching defeat of Japan in World War II and the difficulties that imposed on everyday life. On March 9, 1945, twelve-year-old Yoko was sheltering in a bunker with her family when the city was firebombed by US planes and 100,000 people were killed. After that they fled to the countryside, where they had to barter away family treasures to buy food.

After the war, Yoko enrolled at Gakushuin University to study philosophy—the first woman to do so—though she did not complete the course. The family moved to New York and she began to hang out with artists, musicians, and poets, fascinated by the vibrant arts community of Downtown. One of Japan's wealthiest men had written to her parents asking for her hand in marriage, but Yoko was a rebellious soul and at the age of twenty-three she eloped with a composer, Toshi Ichiyanagi. They moved into a loft in Greenwich Village and she became involved in the Fluxus group of multimedia artists, among whom was the avant-garde composer John Cage. Yoko began designing her own innovative artworks, including one called *Cut Piece* (1964) in which she sat on stage and invited

OPPOSITE
John and Yoko. She was attracted to working-class guys, perhaps in rebellion against her privileged background.

BELOW
Two-year-old Yoko with her father and mother, Eisuke and Isoko Ono, in San Francisco, 1935. Her mother was a beauty whose picture regularly appeared in society magazines.

audience members to cut off her clothes piece by piece.
It was a world in which she felt at home, and the American
reviews of her work were encouraging, but back in Japan the
press was hostile. Why was such a high-born woman making
this strange art? Her marriage broke down in 1962 and, feeling
overwhelmed, she briefly checked into a clinic for a rest, where
she was visited by American filmmaker and art promoter
Anthony Cox, whom she had met in Tokyo the previous year.
They became lovers, got married, and, in August 1963, had
a daughter named Kyoko.

In September 1966, Yoko visited London to attend a
symposium entitled, "The Destruction of Art." She held her
own show in the Indica Gallery and it was there, on November
9, that she first met John when he walked into the gallery while
she was still setting up. One of her artworks invited viewers to
hammer a nail into a white sheet of board. John wanted to do
so, but Yoko stopped him because the show had not yet opened.
She relented and said he could if he paid her five shillings. He
grinned and replied, "I'll give you an imaginary five shillings
and hammer an imaginary nail in." He recalled later, "That's
when we locked eyes and she got it and I got it and that was
it." That wasn't quite it, though—they would have to transcend
a lot of heartache before they could be together.

BELOW
*A key day in the
history of music—The
Quarrymen played at
St. Peter's church fête on
July 6, 1957, where John
met Paul McCartney.
They chatted for about
five minutes and Paul
showed him how to
tune his guitar, which
was in G banjo tuning.*

The roots of genius

John was an angry man, with an acerbic wit and
a low boredom threshold, who happened to be
half of one of the most talented songwriting
partnerships of all time. He was a troubled soul,
who dabbled in drugs and Eastern philosophy
without finding the answers he sought. Since
1962 he had been married to his college sweetheart,
Cynthia, with whom he had a son, Julian, but he
was not engaged in his home life, preferring to
spend time with the other Beatles or with female
fans. Perhaps it's hardly surprising he found family
life so difficult, given his own fractured background.
His father Alf was away at sea most of the time
and his mother Julia was a tipsy, flirtatious
woman who was anything but a reliable parent.
Predictably, Alf and Julia broke up and when
John was five years old, they placed him at the
center of a tug-of-war, asking him to choose which parent
he wanted to live with. At first he clung to his dad, but when
his mom started crying he ran to her. It was a dreadful position
to put a child in, one that caused psychological scars. John
went home with his mom that day, but when she started
"living in sin" with a new man his aunt Mimi successfully
sought custody, and Mimi it was who brought him up in a
home that was orderly if sometimes short on affection.

ABOVE
*John with Cynthia.
"There was nothing
basically wrong with
my marriage to Cyn,"
he said. "I suppose that
me being away so much
during the early years
of our marriage, I never
did feel like the average
married man."*

John was a creative boy who loved drawing cartoons for
the school magazine and playing the guitar. He formed a skiffle
band, The Quarrymen, and invited Paul McCartney to join
them after meeting him at a church fête gig on July 6, 1957.
On leaving school, John went to art college, where he met
his future wife, Cynthia, but he wasn't cut out for studying
and rebelled against any form of authority. In August 1960,
when he was offered a 48-night gig in a nightclub in Hamburg,
he had no compunction about dropping out of college and
heading to Germany with the band (now named The Beatles),
which by then consisted of him, Paul, George Harrison, and
Stuart Sutcliffe, a friend from art school. Their rock 'n' roll
sound combined with the anarchic stage presence of John and
Paul made them a roaring success. Unlike many competitors,

RIGHT
The Beatles in 1964.
"We all looked up to
John," said Paul. "He
was older and was very
much the leader; he
was the quickest wit
and the smartest."

they wrote their own songs, and what's more, they were good.
In the early days John and Paul wrote head to head, but later
they would work out a melody and lyrics on their own before
bringing it to the other for development. All in all, between
1962 and 1969 their partnership gave rise to around 180
songs, many of them classics, such as "A Day in the Life,"
"Hey Jude," and "All You Need Is Love." The help of manager
Brian Epstein and producer George Martin were the final
components needed to make a group that in just a few years
would transform popular music.

But John wasn't happy. Apart from anything else, there had
been many losses in his life. Aunt Mimi's husband George, his
surrogate father, died when he was fourteen; his mother Julia
was knocked down and killed when he was seventeen; Stuart
Sutcliffe died of a brain hemorrhage when John was twenty-
one; and their manager Brian Epstein died suddenly from an
accidental overdose in August 1967, confirming John's sense
of anger at what he saw as the random cruelty of the universe.
He sometimes took out his anger on Cynthia, admitting,
"I was a hitter. I couldn't express myself and I hit." He'd had
dozens of affairs but said, "I'd never met anyone worth breaking
up a happily married state of boredom for." At first he saw Yoko
as just one more possible conquest. In October 1967, after
inviting her to a recording session at London's Abbey Road
Studios, he took her to a nearby apartment and tried to sleep

with her. She was offended at his lack
of respect and declined, but afterward
worried that he would lose interest. Her
marriage to Cox had broken up and she
was very attracted to John. "Up to then
English men had all looked kind of weedy
to me. This was the first sexy one I met,"
she said. She didn't want to lose him.

> **"I'D NEVER MET ANYONE WORTH BREAKING UP A HAPPILY MARRIED STATE OF BOREDOM FOR"**

Hounded by the media

According to Cynthia, Yoko bombarded John with cards and
letters and began calling their home at all hours. She sent
John a book of poems she had written and persuaded him
to sponsor an exhibition of her work entitled *Half-a-Wind*.
In February 1968, when The Beatles flew to India to study
meditation with the Maharishi Mahesh Yogi, Yoko sent him
cards with simple messages such as "Watch for me—I'm a
cloud in the sky." Then, on May 16, 1968, while Cynthia was
on vacation, John invited Yoko to come down to his
house near Weybridge in Surrey. They sat playing
music all night long, writing tracks that would
later be released on an album called *Two Virgins*,
and according to John they "made love at
dawn." Cynthia got home to find them
sitting around in bathrobes. Yoko explained,
"We both knew this was it. We were
both so excited about discovering each
other, we didn't stop to think about
anyone else's feelings."

The press caught on to the
new relationship very quickly and
were hostile from the start. How
could a member of the Fab Four,
who could have any girl he chose,
pick this short Japanese girl with
long dark curtains of hair almost
covering her face? There was overt
racism in the coverage. It was just
twenty-three years since the end
of World War II and memories were

BELOW
*A still from the Two
Virgins shoot. Yoko's
family were scandalized
that she appeared naked
on the front and back
of the album cover.*

WHY JOHN LEFT THE BEATLES

When Brian Epstein died, John predicted the demise of The Beatles because in his opinion Brian had held everything together. They'd given up doing live concerts back in 1966 because the hysterical fans and general mayhem had become terrifying. By the late '60s, Apple Corps, the company they had founded, was hemorrhaging money and John was "sick of being fucked around by men in suits, sitting on their fat arses in the City." He and Paul were moving in different directions musically, and they fell out over the management of the band. Paul wanted the family of his new girlfriend, Linda Eastman, to manage them while the other three preferred to go with the Rolling Stones' ex-manager, Allen Klein. Although outnumbered, Paul refused to sign a contract with Klein. Then in the summer of 1970, John told the others he was leaving—"I started the band. I disbanded it. It's as simple as that"—but they persuaded him to keep it quiet. It was Paul who publicly announced his departure, saying later, "I couldn't just let John control the situation and dump us as if we [were] the jilted girlfriend." The two were at loggerheads for a while but became reconciled once the lawyers were out of the picture.

still vivid of the treatment of British prisoners in Japan's notorious death camps. Yoko soon became a hate figure for Beatles fans, who shouted racist insults in the street. One girl handed her a bunch of yellow roses with the stems thrust toward her so she would prick her fingers on the thorns. When they emerged from court after John had been charged with possession of cannabis, fans mobbed them, one viciously yanking Yoko's hair. Even Aunt Mimi asked, "Who's the poisoned dwarf, John?" Yoko was a strong character, but it must have been soul-destroying to be the target of such vitriol.

For John, she was the person he had been looking for his whole life. "We were two halves and together we are whole," he said, and he proved to be a possessive lover who wanted Yoko with him day and night. He brought her to Beatles recording sessions and asked her opinion on every take, which soon irritated the other band members. Paul tactfully suggested she might stay in the background a little more, while George accused her of giving off "bad vibes." As the era of peace and love drew to a close, there were mounting creative differences as well as legal and practical difficulties putting pressure on the group, and her constant presence certainly didn't help. When John and Yoko staged their honeymoon in 1969 as a week-long "Bed-in for Peace" in an Amsterdam hotel, the press turned up hoping to watch them having sex and were disappointed to find them wearing pajamas and talking about new ways of promoting world peace.

ABOVE
The Amsterdam Bed-In, 1969. For seven days, John and Yoko stayed in bed, eating all their meals there and entertaining the world's press with their antiwar views. "If you want to sell peace, you've got to sell it like soap," John explained.

Yoko later said she hadn't known what John was planning when he told the other three Beatles he was leaving the band in the summer of 1970. She recalled thinking, "My God, those three guys were entertaining him for so long. Now I have to be the one to take the load." Friendships of over a decade crumbled as a sad, difficult time for each band member left them contemplating their musical futures alone.

So much loss

Yoko lost a lot through her relationship with John—any serious consideration of her work by the public, for a start—but the biggest loss of all came in 1971 when Anthony Cox disappeared with their eight-year-old daughter Kyoko after a messy custody battle. Despite the best efforts of the private detectives John and Yoko hired, they couldn't be tracked down. Yoko was now so traumatized she had constant nightmares and couldn't bear to see children of the same age, even on television. She kept buying tiny cashmere sweaters for the girl until years later a friend pointed out that Kyoko would probably have grown bigger than Yoko herself. It would be 1994 before she saw her daughter again, by which time Kyoko was married and had children of her own.

LEFT
A letter from John, George, and Ringo to Lee Eastman, underlining a key area of dispute between Paul and the rest of the Fab Four.

"IN A WAY BOTH JOHN AND I RUINED OUR CAREERS BY GETTING TOGETHER"

John and Yoko moved to New York and made albums with their own group, the Plastic Ono Band, but he was fiercely competitive with the other Beatles. He derided Paul's solo efforts as "granny music," yet was jealous of the huge fortune his former writing partner managed to amass. He was also annoyed that George's first solo album, *All Things Must Pass*, was so successful. "In a way both John and I ruined our careers by getting together," Yoko said in 2012. "Although we weren't aware of it at the time." She led him toward the avant-garde style of music that was more to her taste and away from his commercial hits of the past, and her own work was entirely eclipsed by her infamy as the wife of an ex-Beatle.

By 1973, the pressures of the relationship, John's neediness, and in particular his high sex drive had become too much for Yoko. "I needed a rest. I needed space," she says. She suggested they take a break and sent John to Los Angeles with her pretty twenty-two-year-old assistant May Pang. John began an affair with May but spoke to Yoko on the phone every day and begged to be allowed to come home. She held him at arm's length for eighteen months, until January 1975, when finally she gave him permission to return. She claims their love was deeper as a result of the separation, which they referred to afterward as the "lost weekend." Almost immediately she became pregnant and in October that year their son Sean was born. John was so smitten with this child, and so determined to be a better father to him than he had been with Julian, that he agreed to be the househusband who did the lion's share of childcare. Yoko was in charge of business and handled their finances very astutely with a combination of her own instincts and the advice of the numerous psychics, astrologers, and Tarot-card readers she consulted.

None of her psychics, however, warned Yoko of

OPPOSITE
John's Gallotone "Champion" guitar, the one he was playing the day he met Paul.

BELOW
"When I met John I was self-conscious about my appearance," Yoko confided. "John said to me, 'No, you're beautiful. You don't have to hide your hands, your legs are perfect, tie your hair back, and let people see your face.'"

the catastrophic event that would occur on December 8, 1980. Mark David Chapman, an unstable twenty-five-year-old Beatles fan from Texas, flew to New York after hearing "voices" in his head. John and Yoko had been working in the studio and at around 10:30 p.m. walked back to the Dakota Building where they lived. They were in good spirits, having heard earlier that their *Double Fantasy* album was about to go gold. John had signed a copy of it for Chapman earlier in the day, but the young man was waiting outside the building as they returned. He called out "Mr Lennon" before pulling out a handgun and shooting his idol five times. John managed to stagger into the vestibule, then collapsed. He was pronounced dead on arrival in hospital. The international outpouring of grief was immense. Yoko released a simple statement—"There is no funeral for John. John loved and prayed for the human race. Please do the same for him"—then took to her bed for a long time, keeping her terrible pain out of sight of the watching media.

Now in her ninth decade, Yoko continues to make art and music and to work for peace but has never remarried. She is still the caretaker of John's memory. "He was a very strong and beautiful and protective force for me," she says. "But his words and music are still here ...That's the fate of an artist. It's not a bad one."

IMAGINE

John Lennon composed the music for his best-known song, "Imagine," in early 1971, in an effort to create a spiritual ballad of his own to rival George Harrison's chart-topping "My Sweet Lord," which came out in November 1970. He later admitted that the concept and a lot of the lyrics for "Imagine" came from Yoko: a poem in her book *Grapefruit* called "Cloud Piece" instructed the reader to imagine clouds dripping, and the positive visualizing of a world at peace was very much a part of her methodology. "In those days I was a bit more selfish, a bit more macho, and I sort of omitted her contribution," he said later, admitting it should be credited as a Lennon/Ono song. Upon its release, religious groups were upset by certain lines, such as the one that asked listeners to imagine there being no heaven. John had been in their bad books since his controversial 1966 remark that The Beatles were more popular than Jesus. All the same, "Imagine" got to number three in the US charts and was the best-selling single of John's solo career. After his death, it became an anthem and continues to be covered by other artists and played at significant events.

SERGE GAINSBOURG
& JANE BIRKIN

ROCK 'N' ROLL

LUCIEN GINSBURG

Born: April 2, 1928
Paris, France

Died: March 2, 1991
Paris, France

JANE MALLORY BIRKIN

Born: December 14, 1946
London, UK

★

THEIR NAMES WERE PLASTERED
ALL OVER THE PRESS,
AND SERGE LOVED IT

When Jane first met Serge, each was mourning a recent breakup with a partner they had thought of as the great love of their life. It wasn't a promising start, but before long their relationship had flowered into something extraordinary and life-changing.

Jane didn't speak a word of French when she flew to Paris in 1968 for a screen test for a French movie. As she waited her turn, she heard another actress delivering the lines perfectly and wished she had never come. She needed the work, though, as a single mom with a young daughter to support. Serge Gainsbourg, who was starring in the movie, was offhand with her. "Why don't you ask how I am?" she said, feeling awkward that he was ignoring her, and he replied, *"Parce que ça m'est égal"*—("Because I really couldn't care")—at which she burst into tears (although she didn't speak the language, she caught the gist of his indifference toward her). Against the odds, she was given the part in the movie *Slogan*, but Serge remained distant on set, even during a scene in which Jane had to stand naked while he reclined in a bath. Finally, she asked the director to arrange for them to have dinner together, hoping to thaw his icy exterior, and it turned into the date of a lifetime.

Serge took her from nightclub to nightclub—Russian clubs, transvestite clubs—both of them getting more and more drunk. When she asked him to dance, he stepped on her toes and she realized, first, that he couldn't dance, and, second, that his gruff exterior was actually a mask for shyness. As morning broke, they arrived at the Hilton Hotel, where the receptionist asked Serge if he wanted his usual room. They went upstairs and, while Jane was in the bathroom, he passed out on the bed. She slipped out to a nearby record store and bought the single "Yummy yummy yummy (I got love in my tummy)," which was then in the charts. She stuck it between his toes and made her departure without waking him. And that was their first date.

OPPOSITE
Serge never told any woman that he loved her in so many words—not even Jane. "I feel it, but I don't know how to say it," he explained, "although I love to hear it said."

BELOW
Serge called Jane his "little hermaphrodite." He preferred younger women whom he could mold to fit in with his lifestyle and tastes, and later said of Jane, "As Pygmalions go, she's probably the best I did."

> ## "LITTLE BY LITTLE, WE RUBBED THE OTHER PEOPLE OUT AND BECAME THE PRINCIPAL CHARACTERS IN QUITE ANOTHER STORY"

The affair began and soon both knew they were in love. Jane was scared because in her previous relationship, with the James Bond theme composer John Barry, her insecurities had made her needy and clingy, which had driven him away, and now she feared the same thing would happen again. Serge was eighteen years older than her and the year before he'd had an affair with sex siren Brigitte Bardot, with whom she didn't feel she could compete. He'd also been married to a woman from a very wealthy family who showered him with gifts, including a Steinway grand piano, and Jane couldn't compete with that either. As it turned out, she didn't need to because Serge fell for her just as she was. Jane later explained to Serge's biographer, "Little by little, we rubbed the other people out and became the principal characters in quite another story."

Music in his blood

Serge's parents were Russian Jews who had fled the Communist Revolution and relocated in Paris, where his father earned a living playing piano in clubs and theaters. Having escaped the violence back home, a mere two decades later they were faced with a new menace when World War II began and Paris was occupied by German troops. In 1940 a law was passed that all Jews had to register with the authorities and in 1942 they were ordered to wear a yellow star on their clothing. "It was like you were a bull, branded with a red-hot iron," Serge recalled. The family relocated to Limoges in central France, which was not subject to the Nazi Occupation, but where they were still very much in danger. Once when there was a spot check at Serge's school, a teacher sent him out to hide in the forest so he wouldn't be rounded up and sent to Auschwitz, as had happened to his Uncle Michel.

When the war ended, Serge left school without completing his final exams and enrolled in art college, where he had a passionate affair with a Russian aristocrat called Elisabeth Levitsky. She obtained the keys to Salvador Dalí's Paris home and they let themselves in and made love in the black-walled living room, which greatly impressed Serge. They married in November 1951, at a time when both were working at a school

OPPOSITE
Serge with France Gall at a party to celebrate their 1965 Eurovision win. On the surface, the lyrics of "Poupée de cire, poupée de son" seem like pop nonsense set to a catchy tune, but on closer analysis they talk about how young people turn to pop songs to find out what life's about only to discover they are sung by singers too young and naïve to know.

for Holocaust survivors. By this point, Serge had decided an artist's life wasn't for him and he took up music, working as a bar pianist like his father and studying composition. During the summer seasons at French holiday resorts, he was a magnet for women and after the third such summer, Elisabeth divorced him for adultery. He started writing cynical songs about love—and began, shyly, to sing them in clubs. He changed his name from Lucien, which he thought made him sound like a hairdresser, to Serge, reflecting his Russian heritage; and from Ginsburg to Gainsbourg, after the English painter Gainsborough. A recording contract followed, but his first album, *Du chant à la une!* ("Songs on Page One"), was not a hit. It wasn't until he embraced a style of pop music known as "le yé-yé," designed to target American success (the name deriving from the "yeah, yeah" you might hear in the chorus of an English-language pop song), that he began to have commercial hits. Then his song "Poupée de cire, poupée de son," performed by France Gall, won the 1965 Eurovision Song Contest

EUROVISION

During the 1950s the European Broadcasting Union needed ideas for entertainment programs that could be shown across Europe, and decided to inaugurate a song contest. At the first one, held in Switzerland in 1956, seven countries took part, each submitting two songs. Since then, a total of fifty-two different countries have competed, not all of them strictly part of Europe (Israel, Morocco, Russia, Turkey, and Azerbaijan have all taken part). The entries tend to be cheesy pop songs sung by bands wearing attention-grabbing costumes (either based on national dress or revealing lots of flesh). Serge hated this kind of "baby pop," but swallowed his principles to write "Poupée de cire, poupée de son" (the English version was called "A Lonely Singing Doll") in 1965. France refused it and it became Luxembourg's entry, sung by blonde, sixteen-year-old France Gall. To shrugs of French chagrin, it won. Other notable winners have included Abba with "Waterloo" (1974), Sandie Shaw with "Puppet on a String" (1967), and Céline Dion with "Ne partez pas sans moi" (1988). In recent years the contest has been mired in controversy, with accusations of countries block-voting to favor candidates from their own part of the Continent.

RIGHT
Journalists often described Serge as ugly, yet he managed to seduce Brigitte Bardot, whom many at the time considered the most beautiful woman in the world. "Ugliness has more going for it than beauty does; it endures," he said.

and soon big-name artists including Petula Clark, Sacha Distel, and Brigitte Bardot, were all singing his songs.

His affair with Brigitte began in 1967 after he was invited to appear on her TV show. His second marriage, to the wealthy Béatrice Pancrazzi, had just broken down, and Brigitte's marriage to German playboy Gunther Sachs was on the rocks. By all accounts Serge and Brigitte had a very passionate time together. Her nickname for him was *"guile d'amour"* ("love face"), and he wrote what would become his most famous song for her: "Je t'aime . . . moi non plus." The title, which translates as "I love you . . . me neither," reflected Serge's love of wordplay and double meanings, and the song—like many of his compositions—was all about sex. Brigitte recorded it with him, moaning and sighing as if in the heights of lust, against a backdrop of organ music, but when her husband found out, he forbade her to release it. Serge was devastated when she decided to go back to Gunther and give her marriage another chance. He had loved the kudos that came with being the lover of France's sexiest woman and, apart from anything else, he needed someone to record his song. And then along came Jane.

Je t'aime

Jane was the daughter of actress Judy Campbell, a famous beauty who had been the muse of Noël Coward. Her father was a Royal Navy commander. She grew up on the Isle of

Wight and came to London at the age of seventeen seeking
work as an actress. Jane had the classic Swinging Sixties look,
with a lean, boyish figure and long, straight hair, and although
she was self-conscious about her big teeth and lack of curves,
she let photographer David Bailey take some stunning pictures
of her. In 1965 she was cast in a musical called *The Passion
Flower Hotel* about girls in a boarding school, and she fell in
love with composer John Barry, who had written the music.
He was thirteen years older than her and, she says, had
"a reputation for being mad, bad, and dangerous to know."
This proved accurate when three years later he left her
heartbroken with a young daughter to care for. In the
meantime, she made headlines in 1966 as the first actress to
bring full-frontal nudity to the British screen in the movie
Blow-Up and had also appeared in *Wonderwall* (1968), with
music composed by George Harrison. It was these performances
that brought her to the attention of *Slogan* director Pierre
Grimblat and led to her being cast opposite Serge.

The early days of their affair were joyous. They went to
Venice and sat drinking in Harry's Bar. In Paris they stayed in
Oscar Wilde's old bedroom at L'Hôtel des Beaux-Arts and went

BELOW
*Jane with Serge,
smoking one of his
Gitanes. He loved the
"physiological orgasm"
of smoking, she said,
adding, "Like a child, he
didn't believe anything
serious could happen
to him."*

COURTING CONTROVERSY

Serge was a talented wordsmith who enjoyed playing with sexual double entendres. Jane described his lyrics as "extremely witty and clever, but very cruel and cynical." Following the 1965 Eurovision win, he wrote a song for France Gall entitled "Les Sucettes" ("The Lollipops"). She recorded it but was mortified when it was pointed out to her later that the lyrics, about a girl who is in paradise every time "that little stick" is in her mouth, referred to oral sex. Perhaps his most controversial song, in a career that was chock-full of controversy, was "Lemon Incest," recorded with his daughter Charlotte, the lyrics playing on the phrases "lemon zest" and "incest." The video of them lying together on a bed, her with bare legs and him with a bare chest, created a scandal even when he pointed out that the lyrics speak of a love that will never happen. In 1979, Serge released "Aux Armes Et Caetera," a reggae version of the French national anthem, which led to death threats but still sold over a million copies. The play on words in his songs is ingenious and poetic but makes them difficult to translate, which is probably why he is not better known outside France.

to nightclubs every night. And when she was cast in a movie that was filming in Saint-Tropez, Serge hired a huge limousine to drive her and her daughter down there. He liked her singing voice, which he described as a "choirgirl's voice," and got her to record the theme song for *Slogan* and then the notorious "Je t'aime." When it was released, rumors spread that they had recorded a live sex session, and the warning the record company put on the front cover, that it was for "over-21s only," increased its notoriety. It was banned in Italy after the Vatican cardinals deemed it "an obscenity," it was banned by the BBC in London (and yet it still made number one in the British charts), and it was also banned in Spain and Sweden. Even in France it could not be played before 11 p.m. Their names were plastered all over the press, and Serge loved it.

In July 1971, Jane gave birth to a daughter, Charlotte, and soon afterward they moved into a house Serge had bought at number 5 Rue de Verneuil in Paris. He'd had it decorated with black felt walls (reminiscent of the black walls in Dalí's apartment), had the windows covered because he didn't like daylight, and everywhere there were carefully arranged objects, as if it were a museum. Everything had its place and nothing could be moved. "When I come in I can *feel*, right away . . . if someone has altered my universe," he claimed. Jane had her own room, but he frequently popped in to urge her to keep it tidy. "He wanted to control life," she says. He was an aesthete who told her which dress to wear and how to style her hair when they were going out. In restaurants, he chose what they would eat, and he it was who decided the clubs they frequented and the friends they saw. But she was in thrall to him and for that reason she slotted into the universe he had created. They hired nannies so they could go out most nights, and they tried to arrange her movie work so that he could accompany her on set. "We weren't separated for a week," she says. Everything seemed perfect—until May 1973 when at the age of just forty-five, he had a heart attack.

ABOVE
Jane with Kate (left), her daughter by John Barry whom Serge brought up as his own, and Charlotte. Kids were not allowed to move anything in Serge's house and he was strict about table manners.

Grand gestures

Serge had been a heavy smoker since the age of thirteen, and was such an addict that he smuggled two hundred Gitanes into hospital as he recovered from his heart attack. He was also a heavy drinker, a habit which had started during his compulsory military service and carried on from there. No health scare would make him change the habits of a lifetime, no matter how much Jane pleaded. She was so angry he wouldn't give up smoking after his heart attack that she took it up herself, saying, "I'll kill myself first if that's what the game is." But he was unrepentant. When he was drinking, he could sometimes be rude and hurtful toward her. She always carried around a large basket full of things she felt she needed and one night,

OPPOSITE
"My only contribution to him, apart from inspiring his songs, was telling him not to shave and giving him a diamond to wear around his neck," said Jane. "He had a dandified quality and I thought it so sophisticated to have a diamond against his bare chest."

SHE TOLD HIM SHE WAS DEPRESSED AND, WITH CUSTOMARY ÉLAN AND INSOUCIANCE, HE WROTE A SONG ABOUT IT RATHER THAN TRYING TO HELP

in front of friends, Serge began to empty it out, commenting sarcastically on the clutter, and even tipping out the tampons she kept in the bottom. Humiliated, she decided to get revenge, and a few nights later, when they were drinking with the same crowd and, for some reason, a custard pie had been left on the table, Jane picked it up and threw it in Serge's face. Instead of trying to wipe it off, he stood up and walked out of the club. She ran after him and, by way of trying to make things right, threw herself into the River Seine. The emergency services had to be called to rescue her and Serge waded in to help. It was the most dramatic of their many fights, but, she later mused, "Serge was . . . a fan of the grand gesture."

Serge always believed that Jane finally left him because of the mean things he said and did when drunk, for which he took full responsibility. But in truth, she was tired of "the monotony of coming back at exactly the same time as the [garbagemen] . . . and the children waking up just as you roll in." She told him she was depressed and, with customary élan and insouciance, he wrote a song about it rather than trying to help. Then, in the summer of 1979, she met the movie director Jacques Doillon and moved out of 5 Rue de Verneuil to be with him. She later explained, "I escaped to get out of being the sort of beautiful creature [Serge] wanted me to be. I didn't want to be told what to do any more, or not allowed to touch anything in his sitting room." Serge was distraught, but threw himself into his work—and into the bottle. He was working with actress Catherine Deneuve at the time, who felt sorry for him and visited regularly to check he was all right. Jane still came round with home-cooked casseroles, worried that he wasn't eating properly. Serge continued to write songs for Jane to record, but now they were all about the pain of her leaving him. He bounced back and, by spring 1981, he had a new girlfriend, a model called Caroline von Paulus, known to all as Bambou, but still he kept Jane's room in his house just as it had been when she lived there. When Jane's daughter Lou was born, he sent expensive gifts for the baby and called himself "Papa deux." As breakups go, it couldn't have been more civilized.

Not the end

In 1989, doctors told Serge that
if he didn't stop drinking he would
be dead within a year, and yet he
carried on. He lasted until March 2,
1991 when, at the age of sixty-two,
he had another heart attack and
died in his bed, where Bambou
found him the following morning.
Jane was in England looking after
her sick father but she hurried back
on the first flight and for four days
the women closest to him—Jane
and her daughter Charlotte, Bambou
and Catherine Deneuve—sat in the
bedroom with his body, unwilling to
let him go. Paris came to a standstill
as thousands of fans flocked to pay
their respects outside the house on
the Rue du Verneuil. For several
days, news programs talked
constantly about his achievements
and radio stations played his music.
The French President Francois
Mitterand paid tribute, saying, "He
has raised the song to the level of
art," and Brigitte Bardot said, "We
have lost someone irreplaceable."

ABOVE
*Serge in 1982 with
Bambou, the half-
Chinese, half-German
lover he met in 1981.
Toward the end of
his life, Serge created
a persona called
Gainsbarre who could
say and do outrageous
things on TV—like
burning a 500-franc
note to protest against
the level of income tax.*

Just before Serge's funeral, Jane
got word that her father had died. Her grief over the loss
of the two men at the core of her world was agonizing, and
her relationship with Doillon simply couldn't survive it. She
took an apartment on her own and carried on singing Serge's
songs in shows around France, keeping his legacy alive. And
with equal devotion, their daughter Charlotte undertook to
maintain the Rue de Verneuil house exactly as it had been
when he lived there. Above all, there was gratitude. The
thirteen years Jane spent with Serge had given her a life quite
different from what she had expected—but she wouldn't have
had it any other way.

"WE WERE
KINDRED SOULS . . .
CEMENTEDLY IN LOVE"

JAMES TAYLOR

&

CARLY SIMON

ROCK 'N' ROLL

JAMES VERNON TAYLOR

Born: March 12, 1948
Boston, Massachusetts

CARLY ELISABETH SIMON

Born: June 25, 1945
New York City

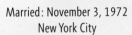

Married: November 3, 1972
New York City

At the age of fourteen, James saw Carly singing in a club in Martha's Vineyard and thought she was gorgeous, but she was three years older than him and he didn't think he stood a chance. Eight years later, when they were introduced by his brother, it was the beginning of a whole new chapter in the annals of rock royalty.

F riends didn't think it would last more than a couple of months when James and Carly hooked up because they were such fragile, complex people, with neuroses (her), addictions (him), and many ton-weights of emotional baggage between them. They came from comfortable middle-class backgrounds, had good educations, and loving, supportive parents, but both had become troubled souls along the way.

In Carly's case, the roots of the damage lay in feeling less attractive and interesting than her two older sisters. She got attention by being funny—"There was never a dull moment when Carly was around," her mother has said—but she lacked confidence and suffered from panic attacks as early as eight years old. She was devastated when her father had a heart attack when she was ten, and said later, "I would knock on wood 500 times every night thinking that would keep him from dying. The fact he didn't die the first night meant I had to keep doing it." She developed a debilitating stammer; when asked to read out in class, she got a lump in her throat that made her gag and the other kids mocked her. From the age of eleven, she was seeing therapists. When she was twelve, her sisters told her that her mother didn't love her father anymore but had fallen in love with someone else, prompting more severe anxiety attacks. And when she was fifteen, Carly's father finally died: "I feared his death incredibly, and I moved away from him fearing that I might die." It affected her later relationships with men; she got into a habit of falling for the wrong types and had her heart broken numerous times.

In James's case, there was a gene for depression and addiction on his father's side, and he was unlucky enough to inherit it. As a child, he was quiet and withdrawn, but intensely musical. It's said he could hold a tune at the age of two and he started cello lessons at ten, then taught himself to play guitar at twelve, with the help of a friend, Danny Kortchmar (aka Kootch). He was

OPPOSITE
"I fell for him right away because he was very easy-going and free-spirited," she said, while he said she was "like a goddess, a goddess of love."

MUSICIANS & MADNESS

Creativity and madness have long been linked, with many artists, writers, and musicians throughout history having suffered a form of mental-health problem. For some it enhances their art, while for others it makes them incapable of working. Brian Wilson, chief songwriter for The Beach Boys, suffered many breakdowns and claims that he began hearing voices in his head after experimenting with LSD. He was unable to work for a long time until a correct diagnosis and suitable medication helped him to resume his career. Syd Barrett, a founding member of Pink Floyd, had a breakdown and left the band in 1968, spending most of the rest of his life as a recluse. Ray Davies of The Kinks and Sinead O'Connor have both spoken publicly about their battles with bipolar disorder. And Ian Curtis of Joy Division succumbed to severe depression and took his own life in 1980, just as the band were preparing for their first US tour, while Kurt Cobain of Nirvana did the same thing in 1994. James Taylor was one of the lucky ones who managed to save himself and channel his pain into writing confessional songs, several of which became all-time classics.

shy around girls but found that being a musician helped to attract them and by the age of fifteen he always had a girlfriend. However, he was falling behind in his schooling and in 1963 his parents sent him to a very strict, all-boys prep school called Milton Academy, which he hated from the start. His parents were arguing a lot and he feared they would separate; he didn't have many friends at the new school, and he was having trouble sleeping. Before long he became desperate and began to contemplate suicide. "I had a lot of emotional problems and I found the toughest thing was just managing to stay alive." After he confessed his suicidal thoughts to his sister, he was referred to a psychiatrist who admitted him to McLean Hospital in Belmont, Massachusetts, an expensive private mental institute. It gave James the respite he needed for seven months, and he finished his high-school education there; it also meant he could get out of serving in the Vietnam War because he was deemed too unstable.

At eighteen he shared an apartment in New York with Kootch and they started a band called the Flying Machine. He wrote songs about his time in hospital, including "Knockin' Round the Zoo," and they signed a deal with a record label. But James's mental-health problems still haunted him, and he found the only reliable way of assuaging his depression was taking heroin. "I just fell into it since it was as easy to get high in the Village [Greenwich Village] as to get a drink." And thus began a habit that would dominate the next decade of his life.

Romance on the rocks

In the summer of 1962, Carly and her sister Lucy, billed as the Simon Sisters, started singing together in the Mooncusser Club on Martha's

Vineyard, where they were watched (though not approached) by a young James Taylor. Carly spent two years studying at the prestigious Sarah Lawrence College in New York's Westchester County but dropped out to concentrate on music after Bob Dylan's manager, Albert Grossman, got her a record deal. He hoped to make her into a female version of Dylan, but her early records didn't make much impact. She had caught the music bug all the same, and kept plugging away through the '60s, taking a job writing jingles for commercials and playing with a band called Elephant's Memory. Her breakthrough came in 1971 with a top-ten hit, "That's the Way I've Always Heard it Should Be," and her second album *Anticipation* reached a wide audience (helped by the fact the title track was used for a Heinz ketchup advert).

Carly was a beautiful, sexy woman with a quick wit, which meant men were always falling at her feet, but the childhood insecurities lingered and inside she often still felt like "the gawky, awkward stutterer." A four-month romance in 1966 with satirical writer William Donaldson, author of *The Henry Root Letters*, left her bewildered and heartbroken. They met on July 8, moved in together on July 20, got engaged, and started buying tea-sets, then on October 24 she received a "Dear John" letter, breaking things off without any proper explanation. She swore off men for a while, but when opening a series of six concerts for Cat Stevens in 1970, she fell deeply in love with him and was shattered when he dumped her. Next she spent six months with Kris Kristofferson, who stopped calling after an occasion when she freaked out on a bumpy flight home following a performance. She also had a fling with Warren Beatty, as she says, before his tally of conquests "had reached, you know, the populations of small countries." She might have seemed to these men like a cool, confident rock chick who could give as

CARLY WAS A BEAUTIFUL, SEXY WOMAN WITH A QUICK WIT, WHICH MEANT MEN WERE ALWAYS FALLING AT HER FEET

ABOVE
The Simon Sisters, Carly and Lucy, performing c.1964. Her ex-fiancé William Donaldson described Carly as "funny, quick, erotic, extravagantly talented."

good as she got, but in fact she was emotionally battered by her experiences. Really, she just wanted to find someone to settle down with, but was going about it entirely the wrong way.

"A certain magical chemistry"

While James was wrestling with on-again/off-again heroin addiction, he managed to build a career as one of the world's most successful solo artists. It began in 1968 during a stay in London when he met Peter Asher, then talent director of The Beatles' Apple label, who took him under his wing. His first album wasn't successful, mainly because the label was in trouble and didn't spend money promoting it, but "Fire and Rain," a song he wrote about a girl he had known in hospital who committed suicide, made number three in February 1970 and the album *Sweet Baby James* was a huge success. James appeared on the cover of *Time* magazine at the age of just twenty-two and he should have been on top of the world—but his mother

BELOW
"I could have easily self-destructed many times but I find my peace and spiritual nourishment in music," James has said.

and father divorced that year, sending him off on yet another drugs bender. In late 1969, he had met singer-songwriter Joni Mitchell and fell madly in love, showering her with love letters and poems he'd written for her, only to fall out of love again, breaking her heart badly.

In April 1971, James's brother Livingston introduced him to Carly Simon, with whom he sometimes played. Both felt "a certain magical chemistry" as they sat and talked. She said later, "It seemed as if we had known each other and lived in the same place before." At the end of the evening, Carly offered, "If you ever want a home-cooked meal . . ." and James replied, simply, "Tonight."

"We never spent a night apart after that," Carly told journalists later. Things got serious very quickly and they were soon discussing what they would call their children. "My love for Carly is a very religious thing," James told a *Rolling Stone* journalist. "I just exchange with her completely and I don't know where I end off and she begins." They stayed in her New York apartment or in a house he had built on Martha's Vineyard, where both had enjoyed childhood holidays. Carly told her mother, "We're madly in love. I finally found the peace and happiness that I've dreamed of finding for so many years."

The problem was that both were at the peaks of their careers and were often required to be on the road or in recording studios on opposite sides of the country for weeks at a time. In the summer of 1972, while she was in London recording the album *No Secrets*, which included the track "You're So Vain," it was reported that Carly was having an affair with Mick Jagger. Bianca Jagger phoned James to tell him about it; Carly denied it and James said he believed her, but on her return to New York, the subject of marriage came up. "There's

YOU'RE SO VAIN

As soon as Carly's song about a self-obsessed lover, "You're So Vain," was released in November 1972, the speculation over who it was written about began. Mick Jagger sang backing vocals on the track, which made him one of the prime candidates. Warren Beatty is reported to have called and thanked Carly for writing a song about him. She assured James it wasn't about him, but everyone had their own pet theory and radio stations even began competitions to nail down the subject through close analysis of the lyrics. In fact, Carly later explained that it began as a song called "Bless you, Ben," then developed at a time when she was feeling angry about all the men who had emotionally used and abused her, before finally coming together when she watched a man she knew walking into an LA party with an arrogant swagger. The final product was hailed by feminists as a woman seizing power and mocking the man who has done her wrong, but it can't have been much fun for James to have everyone speculating over his wife's exes in the month they were married.

"THERE'S NOTHING THAT GETS MEN SO CRAZY AS OTHER MEN PURSUING THEIR WOMEN"

nothing that gets men so crazy as other men pursuing their women," Carly remarked. She and James married in her New York apartment on November 3, 1972, in a rushed and rather basic ceremony. He performed at Radio City Music Hall that night and a huge cheer went up when he told the crowd what they had just done. They'd both been famous before, but now James and Carly became rock royalty, with the media scrutinizing their every move—and just waiting for the marriage to fail.

Marital disharmony

Carly spent a lot of time and energy furnishing their marital home with tasteful possessions, building a nest they could relax in. She told a journalist, "Ours is a relatively comfortable relationship based on our respect and affinity for each other." She was prepared to tone down her party-animal lifestyle and cut right back on touring, which she had never enjoyed because she suffered such severe stage fright. "I wanted to be the little woman behind the man . . ." she said. "I was too shy to be front of stage." She cooked James's favorite meals, kept the house looking nice, threw parties for their friends, and tried her best to be a good wife.

BELOW
James and Carly at a New York party in 1976. His father's advice on their marriage was, "If they want it to work, then they'll both have to tone down their lifestyles considerably."

136

There was one problem she hadn't fully taken account of, though: James's drug addiction. She knew he had a history of heroin use but had no idea quite how deeply he was addicted or what that meant. "It just kind of confused me that there was a wall up between us. I had never been close to anybody who was really addicted to anything before." He had been clean most of the time they were dating, and had even thrown away his drugs paraphernalia, but when he started touring, he got lonely and depressed and did what he always did to take away the pain—shoot up. When Carly realized he'd relapsed, she thought it must be because of her. She found it very difficult to cope with the way he stopped communicating with her, and tried everything she could think of to get through, even threatening to leave him. And then she hit on an idea—surely having children would give him the stability and focus he needed to stay off drugs? She got pregnant and in January 1974 their daughter Sally was born. It worked—for a while. James was a devoted, loving father, telling a journalist that "fatherhood was one of the things that pulled me toward life, as opposed to wanting to lock myself in a refrigerator." But whenever there was any kind of trouble, such as an album that didn't do as well as he'd hoped, the only crutch that helped him was heroin. "I really thought addiction was like a virus, that he would get rid of it," Carly said. "I was in a constant state of denial about it."

She tried to find ways of distracting him when he was troubled, but he would sneak out in the middle of the night to meet his dealer. They lived in Beverly Hills for a time while working on new albums, but neither of them liked it there. James was paranoid about other men lusting after his wife, while she heard rumors of him being unfaithful on tour (untrue according to his bandmates), and there were frequent rows. In 1977 they had

BELOW
In 1981, with their son, Benjamin, and daughter, Sally. By this time there was a rift in the marriage. "It was frustrating," said Carly, "because I loved him so much and I felt like I was up against a brick wall."

a son, Ben, and James was delighted. The same year his album *JT* went double platinum and the single "Your Smiling Face" was a huge hit. He told a journalist that having Ben had "taken my horizon from two months from now to twenty years from now," and said, "I want to spend time with them and feel bad if I don't." But before long he was back on tour, leaving Carly at home with the two children.

In the summer of 1980 Ben became seriously ill with a high fever and rapid weight loss. Carly took him to the best doctors money could buy and eventually he was diagnosed as having a malfunctioning kidney. He had to undergo surgery to remove it and for a while his life hung in the balance. Carly spent all her time at the hospital. "We were both traumatized," she said. "I tend to get hysterical while James is clinical and often tried to escape." In the end Carly felt he failed her during that period because he didn't show his pain on the outside and seemed emotionally absent. Their son survived, but their marriage didn't. They stayed together while Ben recovered, living in the same house but in separate bedrooms, and then in 1983 they got divorced, after eleven years of marriage.

BELOW
Singing together at a No Nukes concert in the summer of 1980, just before Ben became ill. James supports a string of humanitarian causes.

The wall of silence

There was a lot of bitterness in the aftermath of the breakup. Carly called him "an absentee father who cares just about himself." James was said to be very hurt when in 1985 she had an affair with the drummer in his band, while the only contact they had was over the children. He always had the ability to completely cut off from Carly when he chose to and she continued to be hurt that there was no relationship between them any more, just "a long alleyway of memories leading up to a big wall of silence." On the other hand, in 1995 they played together at a concert on Martha's Vineyard and in 1997, when she was diagnosed with breast cancer, he rushed to her

WHEN SHE WAS DIAGNOSED WITH BREAST CANCER, HE RUSHED TO HER BEDSIDE

bedside and did all he could to help her make it through a mastectomy and chemotherapy—before going back to ignoring her again. He has married twice more, to actress Kathryn Walker and then to Caroline "Kim" Smedvig, with whom he had twin boys in 2001. Carly also got married again, to a poet called James Hart.

Looking back on her time with James, Carly said, "I was terribly in love and I got a great deal out of that relationship. I don't think I would have changed anything except that I wish James would have been happier with himself." He had finally got clean in the late '70s and it seems they both helped each other to overcome those early demons. It's a testament to the strength of their love that they managed to spend eleven years together in the media spotlight, when everyone was so sure they wouldn't last more than a couple of months. They were kindred souls, who were, as Carly said, "cementedly in love." And then they weren't anymore.

ABOVE
Carly with her children in 1987 in Martha's Vineyard, "the only place I've ever called home," Carly told a journalist. They continued to live in the house that James had built back in 1969.

IT WAS A GROWN-UP
RELATIONSHIP OF SHARED
INTERESTS AND MUTUAL
RESPECT

LOU REED
&
LAURIE ANDERSON

ROCK 'N' ROLL

LEWIS ALLAN REED

Born: March 2, 1942
Brooklyn, New York

Died: October 27, 2013
Southampton, New York

LAURA PHILLIPS ANDERSON

Born: June 5, 1947
Glen Ellyn, Illinois

★

Married: April 12, 2008
Boulder, Colorado

Lou and Laurie didn't meet until he was fifty and she was forty-five, but almost immediately they recognized each other as kindred spirits. It was a late-in-life relationship that probably wouldn't have worked if they had met any sooner, because Lou first had to learn to tame his many demons.

Lou's father was a tax accountant, his mother a former beauty queen and a stereotypical Jewish mama. The eldest of three children, Lou spent his formative years in Brooklyn before the family moved to Freeport, Long Island when he was eleven. He described his parents as "self-made millionaires," but this was something of an exaggeration. The family were certainly comfortable, and the children went to good schools and had music lessons (Lou learned classical piano). On the surface he was a well-brought-up, well-adjusted middle-class Jewish kid—but it all started to go wrong when at the age of about twelve he realized he was attracted to other boys. He taunted his straitlaced father by adopting an effeminate way of walking and they clashed frequently throughout his teens. His parents were distraught over his claims to be gay and, in 1959, they took what now seems a radical step (but was not uncommon for the day) when they signed Lou into Creedmore State Psychiatric Hospital to have electric-shock treatment designed to make him heterosexual. Three times a week for eight weeks he was strapped down and electrodes attached to his head, with, as he later recalled, a "thing down your throat so you don't swallow your tongue," before an electric shock was administered. Afterward, his hands would be trembling, his memory shot, and he couldn't even sign his own name. When the course finished, he was put on tranquilizers and began weekly sessions with a psychiatrist that continued until 1961 when he headed off to college.

At Syracuse University, Lou found a father figure in Delmore Schwartz, a poet and short-story writer who taught him creative writing, and he also began an affair with a girl called Shelley Albin. But he was still troubled

OPPOSITE
Lou and Laurie—it all started with a computer in Munich in 1992. "She had just gotten this new Mac and was showing it off, and I was impressed by the Mac but I was really looking at her," Lou said in an interview. "Yeah, I knew that," she smiled.

BELOW
Lou, c. 1970. "I was lucky enough to have contact with two geniuses, going from Delmore Schwartz straight to Andy Warhol," he said, crediting both of them for setting him on his musical path.

RIGHT
*The Velvet Underground
with Nico (front left)
and (from left to right)
Lou Reed, Sterling
Morrison, John Cale,
and Mo Tucker. Not
many people bought
their albums at the
time, but it's said that
everyone who did
started their own band.*

and during this period began to take drugs, with numerous
speed and alcohol all-nighters. He let a dealer give him his
first fix of intravenous heroin and later realized he had
contracted hepatitis C from the unsterilized needle used. He
was struggling to find himself, having flings with both men
and women, and when the call-up came to fight in the Vietnam
War, the medical board assessed him as "mentally unfit."

In October 1964, Lou was lucky enough to get a job at
Pickwick Records writing budget-priced songs for radio.
It was a great experience, and led to him meeting classical
musician John Cale, with whom he formed a band called The
Velvet Underground. Andy Warhol, the Pop artist who ran a
New York studio for arty types known as The Factory, took
them under his wing and introduced them to a German model
called Nico who would sing on their groundbreaking 1967
album entitled simply *The Velvet Underground & Nico*. Lou was
an angry young man, though, and it wasn't long before he had
John Cale fired from the band, fell out with Warhol, and then
found himself out on his own, with no band and no manager.
Smarting, Lou went back to Long Island to stay with his
parents, and tried to settle down. He worked in his father's
office and even married a nice local Jewish girl, Bettye Kronstadt.

However, he was fooling himself. He was never going to fit into that particular pigeonhole—or any pigeonhole, for that matter.

Superwoman

While Lou was wrestling with his anger, his homosexual leanings, and his yearning for reality-altering drugs, Laurie Anderson was just graduating from Barnard College, New York City, with a degree in art history. She had grown up in a suburb of Chicago in a big family of four boys and four girls, with pushy parents who forced her to play the violin. She recalls a particularly harsh teacher who said, "If you don't put your fingers in the right places, I am going to put nails where they shouldn't be and you'll prick yourself." At the age of twelve, she had a serious accident while attempting a flip from a high diving board—"I wound up missing the pool and landing on my back"—and the doctors told her she would be paralyzed for life. "That was the first time I realized that adults are idiots," she later said. It took two years to recover, but she spent the time reading classics and developing a love of art. Her parents tried to push her into a career in medicine, but she soon realized she couldn't stand the sight of blood and switched to art history before taking a postgraduate degree in sculpture at Columbia University. In the early '70s she pulled her ideas together to produce her first multimedia performance pieces: *Automotive* (1972) featured lots of car horns creating "music" in an open space; and in *Duets on Ice* (1973) she played her violin while standing in ice skates on a block of ice that was gradually melting. At first she was only well-known in downtown New York among her circle of musician/artist friends, where everyone seemed to be writing operas. "You'd be walking down

HE WAS STRUGGLING TO FIND HIMSELF, HAVING FLINGS WITH BOTH MEN AND WOMEN

BELOW
Laurie performing hits from her debut album Big Science *in 1984. The list of instruments she played on it include vocoder, Farfisa organ, Oberheim OB-Xa, violins, keyboards, marimba, and percussion.*

the street, see a friend and say, 'How's your opera going? Yeah, Mine's coming along too.'" Her fame was spreading, though, and in 1978 she was invited to perform at a convention with William S. Burroughs, Philip Glass, John Cage, Frank Zappa, and Allen Ginsberg, where she stood out in her trademark white suit and punky spiked hairstyle.

In the late 1970s, Laurie met a man to whom she would be close for many years, the comedian and performance artist Andy Kaufman. She saw him performing in a tiny club in Queens, introduced herself and before long found herself being the straight woman in his act. He liked to play with taboos. In one show, for example, he insulted women and announced, "I will not respect a woman until she comes up here and wrestles me down." Right on cue, Laurie would leap up on the stage and have a full-on, realistic fight with him. It was a fun time. Her own repertoire kept expanding as she developed unique musical instruments; altered her voice with cutting-edge technological effects; and included film, dance, mime, poetry, and visual projections in her performances. In 1981, she briefly entered the pop charts, reaching number two in the UK with her record "O Superman," which opened the way to working with international stars such as Peter Gabriel, Brian Eno, and Jean Michel Jarre. There was increasing critical recognition for her work, but she was fiercely independent and not looking for a husband or children. That traditional life choice simply wasn't on her radar.

ABOVE
Laurie playing a tape-bow violin, one of the instruments she invented. It makes a haunting sound that the New York Times compared to "eerie wolf howls."

Coney Island Baby

In 1972, Lou's career was rejuvenated when David Bowie took him under his wing and produced the hit single "Walk on the Wild Side," along with Mick Ronson. It made number sixteen in the US charts and the top ten in Britain, and the album *Transformer* was his most successful ever, but still Lou couldn't help falling out with people. He dissed Bowie in the press, was at loggerheads with his record company, and his marriage to

OPPOSITE
Lou in the Transformer era. Laurie said of his songs that they "are direct and kind of shocking . . . they say things in a very plain, very startling, very beautiful way."

"WALK ON THE WILD SIDE"

The song that became Lou's signature track, "Walk on the Wild Side," is about characters he'd met at Andy Warhol's Factory. There's Holly Woodlawn, a drag queen from Miami who shaved her legs so "he was a she;" there's Joe Dallesandro, an actor and gay sex symbol; Candy Darling, a trans woman (undergoing a sex change from male to female); and the Sugar Plum Fairy, a San Francisco drug dealer. Radio stations in America insisted on bleeping out a reference to "giving head," but the BBC in London played the song, not appearing to recognize that it was about cross-dressing transsexuals shooting so much speed they think they are "James Dean for a day." Lou claimed that "Perfect Day," another track on the same album, *Transformer,* is about a day he spent in Central Park with his first wife, but the rumor spread that it is about two junkies (heroin is what made the day "perfect"). That didn't stop the BBC releasing it as a charity single for Children in Need in 1997, with lines sung by a range of stars including Bono, David Bowie, Elton John, Tammy Wynette, and Laurie Anderson, to name but a few.

Bettye ended as he fell back into hard drug use. And then in 1975 he met "Rachel," a half-Mexican-Indian transvestite whose real name was Tommy Humphries, at a late-night club in Greenwich Village. When Lou spotted Rachel "wearing this amazing makeup and dress," he knew straightaway she belonged "to a different world to anyone else in the place." She moved into his two-bed apartment and they began an intensely passionate three-year relationship, during which they were virtually inseparable. They bought two daschunds, whom they called The Baron and The Duke, and went out for walks with them, Rachel in her leathers and high heels while Lou wore a leather jacket, black jeans, and black shades. At home, they played video games, he messed around on his guitar—and he mainlined heroin. The popular October 1975 album *Coney Island Baby* was a love letter to Rachel, and the track "Nobody's Business" sent out a clear message to the parents who had tried to convert him to heterosexuality.

The punk era of the late 1970s had brought Lou's music new recognition, with many bands citing him and his work with The Velvet Underground as their inspiration. He was the "Godfather of Cool" and relished his new icon status. By the summer of 1978, with friends dying all around him, Lou realized it was time to get himself off drugs. He bought a lakeside house in Blairstown, New Jersey, saying, "Even if you wanted to do something, there's nothing there." But Rachel preferred the city, and inevitably Lou began to drift away from her as he shed his drug habit. Rachel was devastated when they finally broke up.

In 1979 Lou met Sylvia Morales, a British designer, with whom he fell in love. It was a traditional relationship in which she looked after him, cooking, cleaning, and supporting him as he stayed off drugs before managing to quit alcohol, too, in 1981. They married in 1980 and were together for over a decade. Then in 1992, Lou traveled to Munich to take part in a festival to commemorate Kristallnacht, the night in 1938 when the Nazis smashed up Jewish properties, marking the start of the Holocaust. It was organized by avant-garde composer John Zorn, who also introduced him to Laurie. Lou invited her to read out some words while his band played an accompaniment and she was happy to collaborate. Afterward, he told her, "You did that exactly the way I do it." It was a meeting of the minds.

Soul mates

"I liked him right away, but I was surprised he didn't have
an English accent. For some reason, I thought The Velvet
Underground were British," Laurie admits. In fact, they lived
near to each other in New York City. Lou suggested they
got together but she was so busy that it was four months
before they met again at a convention for audio engineers,
which was full of the latest geeky technology both were
fascinated by. The meeting segued into a movie, dinner, and
a walk, and, according to Laurie, "from then on we were never
really apart." They played music together, traveled, made joint
friends, and took up interests such as meditation, kayaking, and
butterfly hunting. He divorced Sylvia in 1993, and he and
Laurie bought a house together in New York's West Village,
while still keeping their own apartments. They had huge
respect for each other's work, and were able to bounce ideas
off each other. "Sometimes it's useful to have somebody else
come in who loves and admires the thing you're working
on, but maybe has a little bit of distance. It's useful to have
someone you can trust, who's on your side," Lou explained.
Naturally, there were compromises to be made and they
sometimes argued. "But," says Laurie, "even when I was mad,
I was never bored. We learned to forgive each other. And
somehow, for twenty-one years, we tangled our minds and
hearts together."

ABOVE
*Lou and Laurie in New
York, 1997. "We loved
our life in the West
Village and our friends,"
she later said, "and in
all, we did the best
we could do."*

ODD SOUNDS & UNUSUAL VOICES

At her *United States II* show in 1980, Laurie premiered a musical instrument of her own design: a violin bow in which the horsehair strings had been replaced with recorded magnetic tape and the violin itself had been strung with magnetic playback heads. The effect was haunting and unsettling, and she continued to update and modify it over the years for other works. Was it perhaps one in the eye for that harsh violin teacher? In the late 1990s, she invented a six-foot-long "talking stick," a MIDI (Musical Instrument Digital Interface) instrument that breaks sounds down into tiny fragments then rearranges and plays them back as she waves it around on stage. She is perhaps best known for the voice filters she uses which deepen her voice to a male register, something she plays with in many shows and albums to analyze the concept of control. She originally called the deeper voice the "Voice of Authority," but when he worked with her on her *Homeland* album (2010), Lou suggested she give her alter ego the name Fenway Bergamot, and the cover showed her with a mustache and thick male eyebrows. He was the expert on blurring genders, after all.

In spring 2008, when Laurie was on tour in California, Lou called her from New York and while chatting she mentioned the things she had never done. "I never learned German, I never studied physics, I never got married." Lou replied, "Why don't we get married? I'll meet you halfway. I'll come to Colorado. How about tomorrow?" They tied the knot in a friend's garden in Boulder, Colorado and she flew straight off again to give a concert that night. It brought a new tenderness to their relationship, she said. It had been a long search, but at last they had each found their soul mate.

And then, in 2011, Lou began to get sick from the hepatitis C he had contracted from a shared needle back in the early 1960s. He had chemotherapy but still developed liver cancer as well as diabetes. Laurie accompanied him to the endless hospital appointments and, although feeling awful, he pursued many projects during this time. He did two hours of tai chi every day, and also studied meditation under a Tibetan Buddhist teacher called Mingyur Rinpoche. He took photographs,

read books, wrote, played, and listened to music, all the while fighting his illnesses. In May 2013, he had a liver transplant and at first was confident it had worked because his energy came back straightaway, but by late summer the transplant had begun to fail and doctors told him there were no further treatments left. Laurie was holding him in her arms when he died, and she says his hands were shaping a tai chi form with his last breath. She wrote her own personal obituary for him. "Lou was a prince and a fighter and I know his songs of the pain and beauty in the world will fill many people with the incredible joy he felt for life. Long live the beauty that comes down and through and onto all of us."

They'd had twenty-one years together, the last and the best years of Lou's life, when he was free from drugs and had resolved the conflicts he'd had with his sexual identity. Laurie was his equal, a fellow artist rather than a wife who stayed home and kept house. It was a grown-up relationship of shared interests and mutual respect. She has described herself as "stunned and grateful" for the miracle of their love.

OPPOSITE
Laurie in New York, 2010, performing Delusion, *a multimedia show featuring her alter ego, Fenway Bergamot.*

BELOW
Laurie and Lou at the 2010 Coney Island Mermaid Parade. In his last interview, Lou talked about sound. "You grow up from when you're a peanut, listening to rhythm. But then there are nature sounds . . . The sound of the wind. The sound of love."

DEBBIE HARRY

&

CHRIS STEIN

ROCK 'N' ROLL

DEBORAH ANN HARRY

Born: July 1, 1945
Miami, Florida

CHRISTOPHER STEIN

Born: January 5, 1950
Brooklyn, New York

★

"HE'S SANE WHERE I'M CRAZY AND
I'M SANE WHERE HE'S CRAZY"

Debbie and Chris thought they were the luckiest people alive to have a partnership that was both creative and romantic, and a band that rode the top of the charts for five years. But at the height of their fame he collapsed and was found to have a rare, life-threatening illness.

Debbie's birth mother got pregnant during World War II as the result of an affair with a man who had omitted to tell her he was already married and had seven or eight children. Quite a big omission. She was heartbroken when she found out and felt adoption was her only option. A New Jersey couple, Catherine (known as Cag) and Richard Harry, took on the baby girl at three months old and gave her a loving home in the suburbs. Debbie was a beautiful baby, of whom her adoptive mom once said, "Friends used to tell me I should send her picture in to Gerber's [the baby food manufacturers] because she would be picked as one of the Gerber babies. But I didn't send it. I didn't believe in her being exploited." Debbie was an imaginative child, who claims to have had her first psychic experience at the age of three or four, when she heard voices coming from inside a fireplace intoning some complex mathematical formulae. And she loved singing. "When I began singing with the radio, I was struck by the fact I knew the next note before it was played."

As a teenager she began to rebel, wanting all her clothes to be black and dyeing her hair every color under the sun. At the age of fourteen, she first bleached her hair, using a peroxide and ammonia mixture that turned it

SHE WAS DELIGHTED WHEN AN AUNT SAID SHE LOOKED LIKE MARILYN MONROE

"a sunny orange color." She loved makeup and penciled beauty marks all over her face, making her look "mud-spattered," as she later admitted. She was delighted when her aunt told her she looked like Marilyn Monroe because she loved the glamor of Hollywood. She knew she was adopted and fantasized that Marilyn might be her real mother. School was the only downside; she "didn't like the pressure . . . that sinking feeling in my stomach," but loved going to dances with her friends and being "a rock 'n' roll teenager." She made out with boys in the backs of cars but only those in a

OPPOSITE
Debbie wrote in her 1998 autobiography, Making Tracks*: "Chris thinks I'm definitely an alien because I fit the description in a book he read of a race of females who were put on this planet from space."*

ABOVE
A brown-haired Debbie, aged about 23, with the band Wind in the Willows, which took its name from the Kenneth Grahame novel. She sang backing vocals and played guitar.

neighboring town, so that she didn't get a bad reputation at home.

After a couple of years at college, Debbie moved to New York and played in bands—the Tri-Angels, Wind in the Willows—while supporting herself by working as a waitress in a nightclub called Max's Kansas City. She got to serve cool people, like the band Jefferson Airplane and the whole Andy Warhol crowd, but success wasn't coming fast enough. She took a job as a Playboy bunny and started getting into drugs, but the highs soon stopped being fun. "After a while, paying for the drugs and doing them became a bigger drag than the problems I was trying to solve." She had a couple of bad experiences with men—she later realized she had been lured into a car driven by the notorious serial killer Ted Bundy and was lucky to escape with her life; there was also a sleazy real-estate broker at her studio apartment who intimated she could stay rent-free in return for sexual favors. Depressed, she moved back home with her parents at the age of twenty-five to try and decide what to do with her life.

Friends first

Chris also struggled with depression, and ended up in a mental institute at the beginning of 1969, just after his nineteenth birthday. His parents were both artistic types—his mother a beatnik painter, his father a salesman and frustrated artist—and he was brought up in the Jewish faith. Chris loved music and got his first guitar at the age of eleven, but his main childhood ambition was to be an Egyptologist. His father died suddenly when he was fifteen and a few years of teenage rebellion followed. He joined neighborhood bands and there were always kids round the house smoking pot. One neighbor smashed their door with a hammer, so irate was he when Chris played the Donovan hit "Sunshine Superman" ten times in a row.

He was thrown out of his school for having long hair, and his mother moved him to a private school in New York called Quintanos, where he persuaded some friends to play with him in a band they called The Morticians. During the summer of 1967, the so-called Summer of Love, he was at the heart of all the hippie happenings in San Francisco and consuming his fair share of drugs. The nervous breakdown in early 1969 happened after he had taken a lot of LSD, but it could also have been in part a delayed reaction to his father's death; at least it had the fortuitous side effect of getting him out of service in the Vietnam War. After his release from hospital, Chris enrolled at New York's School of Visual Arts to study photography and began making friends in the music and arts scene who would gradually, step by step, lead him into the same sphere as Debbie.

She had begun training at a New Jersey beauty school and got a job in a friend's salon, but she still commuted into New York regularly to catch up with friends. One friend, Elda Gentile, invited her to join a band called The Stilettos, and she later said, "If I didn't try, I would never forgive myself. Only singing could give life to that mood, that minute, that was me." They played gigs in the Boburn Tavern on West 28th Street, a tiny bar on the first floor of Elda's apartment block, where they were allowed to perform in the pool room at the back. Chris had become friends with Eric Emerson, who had a band called the Magic Tramps, and who'd also had a son with Elda. That's how Chris was invited to the second-ever Stilettos gig at the Boburn Tavern in 1973, where he met the very beautiful Debbie. At the time she was being stalked by a possessive ex-boyfriend from New Jersey and Chris offered to keep an eye on her, as a friend. It was a wise move. Debbie was used to every straight guy she met trying to hit on her, so the offer of male friendship was a novelty. "He didn't

BELOW
Debbie as a Playboy bunny. "I was really oversexed," she says of her younger years. "Really overcharged and hot to trot."

ABOVE
Debbie was never interested in getting married—or, for that matter, doing anything that was expected of her—but the relationship with Chris was as passionate and loving as it was creative.

have an extreme macho attitude and we had fun together," she recalled. "We laughed at the same things, yet we had differences of opinion and respect for each other."

At the time, Chris was dating a girl called Elvira, an ex-girlfriend of Billy Murcia of the New York Dolls. Debbie had had a fling with the band's singer, David Johansen. If they hadn't met one way, they'd have met another—or they'd have bumped into each other at CBGB, the club where everyone who was in a band used to hang out. The friendship phase of their relationship lasted around three months before the passion took over. Chris broke up with Elvira, joined the Stilettos as guitarist, and he and Debbie moved in together. He later admitted that there may have been an element of calculation in the way he hung back at first, thus gaining her trust, but he was also a man who preferred women's company to men's. The gradual, almost organic start to their relationship was exactly what would make it so strong in the long run.

OPPOSITE
Paul Zone of glam-punk band The Fast, with Debbie and Anya Phillips, founder of the Mudd Club, at CBGB in 1977. David Byrne name-checks both the Mudd Club and CBGB in the Talking Heads song, "Life During Wartime."

The Blondie years

Both Chris and Debbie were well-attuned to what was happening in the worlds of music, art, and fashion in New York in the mid-1970s. Chris in particular had a good ear for where the music scene was heading as the New York Dolls, The Velvet Underground, and the Stooges spawned the Ramones and Talking Heads, and a sound that would become known as "punk" was born. "The style of music was different, the politics were changing . . . a lot of things were changing, and we were right there doing it," Chris said later. He listened to Debbie's "little nasally voice" and thought, "if you double-track that voice, it would be a very interesting effect." In 1974 they formed a new band they called Angel and the Snake, with Debbie on vocals and Chris on lead guitar, but they soon changed the name to Blondie and brought in a drummer, keyboard player, and bass guitarist (by 1975, these would be Clem Burke, Jimmy Destri, and Gary Valentine). They played CBGB but weren't taken very seriously at first because individually none of them were great musicians. They just worked as a band.

CBGB

Entrepreneur Hilly Kristal had managed the Village Vanguard jazz club in Greenwich Village in the 1950s and he bought a place on the Bowery in New York's Lower East Side, planning to turn it into something similar. From 1969 to '72 he ran a bar there, but in December 1973 decided to open CBGB as a home for country, bluegrass, and blues musicians (the name came from the initial letters). Entrance cost $2 to a venue that inside was a complete mess, with indescribably filthy toilets. Kristal booked his first rock act, a local band called Squeeze, in February 1974, and Debbie and Chris played there as The Stilettos, Angel and the Snake, and finally Blondie. The only rules were that bands had to write their own material rather than doing cover versions, and they had to carry their own equipment. The Ramones arrived in August 1974, then Talking Heads the following year, and soon CBGB was the New York home of the growing punk movement. During the '80s it attracted a hardcore punk crowd for its Sunday matinees. The club closed in October 2006, but by then its name had been immortalized in many movies and songs about New York in the '70s.

Part of what got them noticed was Debbie's stage persona, almost a cartoon character of a Marilynesque blonde bombshell singing in a zombie-like voice. She was cooler and more glamorous than other female punk rock stars and became a sex symbol despite (or perhaps because of) the fact that she was in her thirties, which made her a decade older than the majority of punk band members. She explains, "The initial idea was to be desirable, feminine, and vulnerable, but a resilient, tenacious wit at the same time rather than a poor female sapped of her strength by heartthrobs and unrequited love."

Chris and Debbie began to write songs together, with her responsible for 80 percent of the band's lyrics, and they moved into an apartment in Thompson Street, SoHo, which had previously been a doll factory (and which Debbie was convinced was haunted). It was an easygoing relationship based on their shared love of music. They were equals, "very simpatico," according to Debbie, and there were no clashes of ego. Their first album, *Blondie*, came out in 1976, but didn't set the world on fire. Then the band became more widely known after Debbie featured in the fourth edition of *Punk* magazine, naked but holding a guitar, in a tasteful shot taken by Chris. They supported Iggy Pop on tour in 1977, a single, "In the Flesh," made number two in Australia that year, and their second album, *Plastic Letters*, released in 1978, reached number

BELOW
Blondie (from left to right): Gary Valentine, Clem Burke, Debbie, Chris, and Jimmy Destri. According to Iggy Pop, he and David Bowie both tried to hit on Debbie: "We didn't get anywhere but she was always very smooth about that."

ten in the UK album charts. Producer Mike Chapman was brought in to help craft their work for the US market, and Chris has since admitted, "he certainly helped us to pull it together musically." They also signed up with a manager, Peter Leeds, in 1977, agreeing to a type of contract that was common at the time, in which he had power of attorney over their earnings. It was something they would later bitterly regret, but at the time life was becoming all too fast-paced and frantic for them to pay much attention to details.

A string of hits including "Heart of Glass," "Sunday Girl," "Dreaming," and "Rapture" were released in a golden period lasting from 1978 until 1981, when they couldn't put a foot wrong and when they seemed to go straight from one tour to the next. There was a world tour right through the winter of '77 to '78, with a US tour hot on its heels, and by 1979 they were topping the charts on both sides of the Atlantic. It would have been hard for Debbie and Chris to cope with the pressure if they hadn't had each other, but their relationship was strong and very supportive. "Chris and I balance each other out," Debbie explained. "His logic never fails to put things in perspective for me . . . He's sane where I'm crazy and I'm sane where he's crazy." However, both got a little too crazy in the early '80s when the pressures of success led them to dabble in hard drugs, including heroin. "Everyone was doing it so it didn't seem too much of a problem," Debbie said later. "It always starts as a party thing, as a social thing, but then, because it is addictive, it takes over and that's when it interferes with what your main interests are."

In sickness & in health

By the early '80s, there were creative tensions within the band, usually with Chris and Debbie in one camp set against the others. Debbie released a solo album, *KooKoo*, and fulfilled a childhood dream by acting in movies (*Union City,* 1980; *Videodrome,* 1983). Blondie had broken with their first manager in 1979 only to find they owed huge amounts of money to the Internal Revenue Service. "It was a period when musicians still lived in a state of serfdom," explains Stein. "I had a horrendous tax debt for about twenty years. I try not to feel bitter. Debbie keeps reminding me that it's our own fault and we should have

DEBBIE HARRY STYLE

When Chris first met Debbie she had short brown hair and wore thrift-store combinations such as a 1940s floral dress with cowboy boots. Soon after meeting him she bleached her hair and grew it, developing those trademark black roots. Designer Stephen Prouse gave her a pair of thigh-length boots with three-inch heels and persuaded her to team them with miniskirts or mini-dresses he designed for her, creating the iconic "Blondie" look. Debbie was also known for wearing vintage T-shirts with leggings, oversized men's blazers, and chunky 1940s sunglasses. When she got tired of black, she segued into Pop Art colors, worn in asymmetrical dresses or catsuits, some designed by disco-style designer Halston. One of her favorite things was to wear a wedding dress on stage and rip it apart with scissors to reveal a sexy little black dress underneath. She was never going to be the marrying kind, she says, because back when she grew up marrying meant promising to obey some guy, and she couldn't ever see why she would want to do that.

paid better attention [to the agreements they had signed]." Infighting continued and Debbie and Chris agreed to make one last album, *The Hunter* (1982), before the band went their separate ways.

By the time the album was released, Chris had begun to suffer from blisters on his lips and inside his mouth, and they realized he had lost a lot of weight, dropping from 175lb down to 145lb. After he collapsed following a show, he was diagnosed with pemphigus vulgaris, a rare and very serious condition in which the body's immune system starts attacking healthy tissues and painful blisters form on the skin both inside and out. Chris was admitted to hospital immediately for treatment with heavy-duty steroids. The record company wanted to play up his illness for publicity but the idea was anathema to the couple. Blondie could perhaps have continued without Chris, but there was no band without Debbie and she made it very clear that her place was by Chris's side for as long as it took. "It didn't seem like a

sacrifice at all," she says, "because . . . we've always worked as a team." She slept in a cot by his bed, and when he couldn't swallow solid foods she fed him baby food through a straw.

It was four years before Chris felt well enough to play music on stage again, and ten years before he got his energy levels back up. He and Debbie both did rehab to quit drugs and he now says, "I spent . . . years going to the shrink to figure out why I got stoned for all those years and did all that stuff. I needed to deal with that baggage." He adds, "We all went nuts after [Blondie] broke up. Debbie sort of got it out of her system early on but it took me a much longer time." They were still a couple, but at some point during the early 1990s the romance element gradually fizzled out while the friendship grew stronger than ever. When he started dating actress Barbara Sicuranza then married her in 1995, Debbie admits she was jealous at first, thinking, "Who is this woman? Is she good enough for him?" She and Barbara had to work out "where we stood with each other and where each of us stood with Chris." But they found they got on and Debbie became godmother to their two daughters.

Blondie's fans had never deserted them, and in 1996 Chris suggested re-forming. It took him a while to persuade the others, but the following year they played three concerts, then in 1999 released a new album, *No Exit*, from which the single "Maria" made it to number one in the UK, meaning they'd had number ones in three consecutive decades.

Sometimes couples in bands become competitive with each other during their years in the limelight, but Debbie and Chris remained very close throughout. He now says, "being successful with the band helped our relationship rather than the reverse." Debbie agrees: "We were really lucky to meeteach other and have this great adventure."

"WE WERE REALLY LUCKY TO MEET EACH OTHER AND HAVE THIS GREAT ADVENTURE"

BELOW
Chris and Debbie in 2004 after the launch of an album called The Curse of Blondie. *He has said of Debbie, "I think she doesn't even see how much influence she's had."*

SID VICIOUS

&

NANCY SPUNGEN

ROCK 'N' ROLL

JOHN SIMON RITCHIE

Born: May 10, 1957
London, UK

Died: February 2, 1979
New York City

NANCY LAURA SPUNGEN

Born: February 27, 1958
Philadelphia, Pennsylvania

Died: October 12, 1978
New York City

★

"WE KNEW WE WERE MADE FOR
EACH OTHER, AND FELL IN LOVE
WITH EACH OTHER IMMEDIATELY"

Everyone hated Nancy, blaming her for introducing Sid to heroin and dragging him down into the gutter, but really she was just a vulnerable young girl with serious mental-health problems whose only goal in life was to get a rock-star boyfriend.

According to her mother, Nancy came into the world "kicking and screaming at some unseen enemy," and she continued screaming from that point on: "I know it's normal for babies to scream, but Nancy did nothing *but* scream," Deborah Spungen said. She was only twenty years old and her husband Frank was a traveling salesman, so Deborah bore the brunt of dealing with this disturbed baby. When Nancy was three months old, a pediatrician prescribed a sedative but still the distressing behavior continued. At school she was well above average intelligence and was even able to skip a grade, but she found it difficult to make friends. At home she was violent toward her younger brother and sister and threatened to kill a babysitter with a pair of scissors and to hit her mother with a hammer. "We gave in to her," Deborah says, "because there was absolutely no peace in the house until she got what she wanted." She consulted doctors, psychologists, anyone she thought might be able to help, and Nancy was finally diagnosed as schizophrenic when she was eleven, though the family were not told of this diagnosis for another four tortured years.

Nancy was expelled from her school aged eleven and sent to Devereux Glenholme School in Connecticut, a boarding school for children with mental and physical health challenges. Her parents simply couldn't cope with her at home anymore, and were worried about the effect her behavior was having on her siblings. She ran away at fourteen and attempted suicide by slitting her wrists, but was found in time and treated. In 1974 she graduated from high school and enrolled at the University of Colorado aged just sixteen, but was soon expelled for buying marijuana and storing stolen goods. Nancy made her way to New York where her parents paid the rent for a basement apartment in Chelsea. They hoped she would settle down and get a job, but instead she stole money from them and began consuming and dealing in drugs. "It seemed as if every week

OPPOSITE
Sid wrote to Nancy's mother: "I gave her the love she needed so badly and it comforts me to know that I made her very happy during the time we were together."

SHE WAS MOCKED AND NICKNAMED "NAUSEATING NANCY"

she got wilder, further and further from our control and sense of right and wrong," her mother wrote in a book about her daughter. "Our morality meant zero to her."

Nancy's one interest was music. She had a passion for rock 'n' roll and quickly gained an encyclopedic knowledge of the bands playing in clubs like CBGB and Max's Kansas City. She used her drug contacts to meet the musicians and, if she could, she slept with them. She'd have sex for money, for drugs, or just because someone was in a cool band such as Aerosmith, the New York Dolls, the Heartbreakers, or the Ramones. She wanted to be part of the in-crowd, but instead she was mocked and nicknamed "Nauseating Nancy" by the other groupies who hung around the scene. Nancy bragged about the men she'd had sex with; it made her feel she was accepted in some way—but of course she wasn't. No one knew she was schizophrenic. No one cared to ask anything personal about her; she was simply being used as a commodity, a purveyor of sex and drugs.

Being Vicious

The boy who would become Sid Vicious, the most notorious punk musician of the late '70s, was the son of a Buckingham Palace guardsman who also played jazz trombone. Named John Ritchie, when he was a toddler his mother, Anne, took him to Ibiza thinking her husband would join them and the family would live there, but he didn't come and the marriage broke up. She took John back to England where she entered a brief marriage with a man called John Beverley, who died of cancer when her son was eight. Anne then moved to London and left John in the care of her landlady while she worked nights in a jazz club. It was an exhausting life as a single mom and somewhere along the way she became a heroin addict. John was a rebellious boy, whose mother's lifestyle obliged him to move from school to school. After high school he studied photography at Hackney Technical College, where he became friends with future bandmate John Lydon, but he lasted only two semesters before dropping out. Aged seventeen he took to hanging around London's Kings Road, where Vivienne Westwood and Malcolm McLaren had a boutique called SEX,

OPPOSITE
A photo shoot at SEX, on London's King's Road, with, from left to right, Steve Jones of the Pistols, screenwriter Alan Jones with an unknown girl, Chrissie Hynde, Jordan (one of the store assistants), and designer Vivienne Westwood.

which sold punk clothing and accessories. Lydon described John as "a clothes hound" at this time. The two of them would sometimes busk to earn money, but were such terrible musicians that passers-by would pay them to shut up. John, who could only play the tambourine, acquired his stage name "Sid Vicious" after being bitten by Lydon's hamster and exclaiming, "Sid is really vicious." Lydon was supposedly given the name "Johnny Rotten" because of the state of his teeth.

In mid-1976 Sid became lead singer in a band called The Flowers of Romance, and he also played drums for Siouxsie and the Banshees, but his musical career was interrupted after he was imprisoned in Ashford Remand Centre for throwing a glass on stage

PUNK FASHION

Punk was a deliberate rejection of middle-class consumer values, so in the early days clothes tended to be dirty, ripped, second-hand, and generally unkempt. New York musician Richard Hell is often credited as the originator of the spiked hairstyle and the fashion for ripped clothes held together with safety pins. Malcolm McLaren took these ideas back to the UK and introduced deliberately ripped clothing along with bondage gear in SEX, the boutique he ran with Vivienne Westwood. A spiked dog collar worn around the neck, offensive slogans on T-shirts, leathers, chains, tattoos, and multiple piercings were all part of the look. Women wore ripped fishnet stockings along with ballet tutus and motorcycle boots, or rubber fetish gear. Some fans felt the punk movement had lost its way when designers such as Westwood, Jean-Paul Gaultier, and John Galliano produced their own punk designs priced way out of reach of the disaffected working classes the movement had aimed to represent, but the look was here to stay and continued to be influential through subsequent decades.

at a gig by The Damned, which shattered and blinded a girl
in one eye. Back in 1975, Johnny Rotten had joined the Sex
Pistols, along with lead guitarist Steve Jones, bass player Glen
Matlock, and drummer Paul Cook. Managed by Malcolm
McLaren, they were forging a reputation as the band at the
forefront of the British punk movement, with an antiestablishment
philosophy that appealed to the disenfranchised youth of
mid-1970s England, who faced unemployment and, it seemed,
few career prospects. Glen Matlock decided to leave the band
in February 1977 and Sid, by now freed from the remand
home, was invited to take his place. There was a problem in
that he couldn't play bass, but he looked the part with his
filthy spiked hair, his ripped T-shirts, his curled-lip snarl, and
his aggression: "If Johnny Rotten is the voice of punk, then
Vicious is the attitude," McLaren said.

Sid played his first gig with the Pistols in April 1977, around
the time Nancy Spungen arrived in London. She'd gone there
in hot pursuit of Jerry Nolan of The Heartbreakers, on whom
she had a crush, but he refused to see her and she went
to a Pistols gig instead. At first it was Johnny
she wanted to bed, as she later confessed:
"I slept in the same bed as John for two
nights and he said to me, 'You want it
but you're not going to get it.'" So she
turned her attention to Sid, and he was
dazzled. He was sexually inexperienced
but, as Nancy later told a journalist,
she "taught him everything he needs
to know . . . I've put that sexual aura
into Sid." She was highly intelligent—a
dominant, thick-skinned character—and
if people didn't like her because she
spoke her mind, surely that was
all part of the punk ethos?
They were two damaged
people who fell headlong
into a passionate, obsessive
relationship, and soon they
couldn't bear to spend
a second apart.

BELOW
"I'm not vicious really.
I consider myself to be
kind-hearted. I love my
mum." Sid in his clothes-
junkie days.

Mission to self-destruct

"When we first met," Sid wrote to Nancy's mother, "we knew we were made for each other, and fell in love with each other immediately." All her life, Nancy had suffered from terrifying nightmares, but Sid would hold her tight in his arms to help her sleep. He recognized her mental anguish and knew that she was "just a poor baby, desperate for love." In his own version of a love letter, he wrote a list entitled, "What Makes Nancy So Great By Sidney," and among the twelve qualities on the list were "Is extremely smart," "Makes extremely interesting conversation," and "Even has sexy feet." He'd already dabbled in a mixture of drugs, some of them supplied by his junkie mother, but according to friends it was Nancy who first introduced him to heroin, to which she herself was heavily addicted. Sid denied this, telling *NME* "I've been doing every-fuckin'-thing they reckon she turned me onto two years before I met 'er."

He hadn't been involved in the recording of the Pistols' notorious single "God Save the Queen," released in May 1977, but benefited from the band's overnight fame when it shot to number one in the *NME* singles chart despite being banned by the BBC. He also didn't have much to do with the album *Never Mind the Bollocks, Here's the Sex Pistols*, which came out in October 1977, because he spent part of the time it was being

ABOVE
Sid, Paul Cook, Johnny Rotten, and Steve Jones at the shoot for the "Pretty Vacant" video. The song was notorious for Johnny's pronunciation of the word "vacant" with the emphasis on the last syllable.

ABOVE
Iggy Pop said of Nancy, "I spent the night with her. She wasn't a beauty but I liked her. There was something really spunky there."

recorded in hospital with a bout of hepatitis caught from using an unsterilized needle. The two tracks on which he did play had to be overdubbed later because his playing was so bad. But he was still a key band member because his aggressive, don't-give-a-damn attitude personified what punk was about and made him a figurehead for fans.

Johnny Rotten and Malcolm McLaren both believed that Nancy was a terrible influence on Sid. "We did everything to get rid of Nancy," Johnny said later. "She was so fucked up and evil . . . She was killing him." Some compared her to Yoko Ono, who had been accused in 1970 of causing the breakup of The Beatles, but in fact the Pistols were falling apart anyway because of deteriorating relations between Malcolm and Johnny. When the band started an American tour in January '78, Nancy was banned from coming along, but even without her, Sid's violent behavior and his dependence on heroin were worsening. In Texas he hit an audience member over the head with his guitar, and everyone was shocked when he carved the words "Gimme a fix" into his chest. After a show in San Francisco's Winterland Ballroom a couple of weeks into the tour, Johnny announced he was quitting the band, telling the audience, "This is no fun—at all."

Back in London, Nancy decided that Sid should start a solo career with her as his manager. She was a bossy mother figure who convinced him that he had been the talented one in the Pistols and had a big future ahead of him. They played some

gigs in the Electric Ballroom under the name The Vicious
White Kids then in August '78 they flew to New York, where
Nancy was triumphant that she could show off her famous
rock-star boyfriend to all the groupies who used to be so mean
to her. The couple moved into the Chelsea Hotel and she
began to book appearances for him. Large crowds attended his
few shows at Max's Kansas City, but the performances were
dreadful—he mumbled the words and was so stoned he was
barely able to stand upright. He and Nancy had money in their
pockets from his time in the Pistols and the fee for the few gigs
he was able to perform, and they used it to buy street drugs
like kids running riot in a candy store. As well as heroin, they
developed a taste for a sedative called Tuinal and a synthetic
morphine called Dilaudid. With all those substances coursing
around his veins, Sid was never going to be a success as a rock
star. At one point they both signed in to a methadone clinic in
an attempt to beat their dependency, but it didn't work, and
their relationship became increasingly violent—they beat each
other and burned each other with cigarettes. On October 11,
Nancy bought Sid a five-inch hunting knife with a jaguar
carved into the handle. He had other knives, which he claimed
were for protection from crazed fans, but this was a particularly
attractive one. It was the last thing she would ever give him.

BELOW
*Sid and Nancy with Rat
Scabies, drummer with
The Damned, in 1978.
"Sid and Nancy were
going down the toilet
and everyone could see
it," said a friend.*

WHO KILLED NANCY?

Johnny Rotten never believed that his old friend and bandmate murdered Nancy, saying to journalists, "Sid isn't capable of killing her . . . It's not possible," and most of Sid's friends seemed to agree. One theory is that her death was the result of a robbery because the stash of money Rockets Redglare claimed to have seen in the room was never found. Could it have been stolen by the dealer known as "Steven?" Or another dealer who wandered in after he left, fighting with Nancy before picking up the cash? Was she murdered by a member of a Puerto Rican gang she is alleged to have argued with the previous day? In her memoir about her daughter, *And I Don't Want To Live*, Deborah Spungen explains her belief that Sid stabbed Nancy, but only because she told him to, which made it tantamount to a form of suicide. Nancy could even have stabbed herself, or could have fallen onto the knife during a scuffle. Sid confessed to her murder and spoke of their suicide pact, but he was so deeply drugged that night anything could have happened, and he died before the case could come to trial.

RIGHT
Sid was arrested for assault on December 9, 1978, in violation of the terms of his parole.

Murder or a suicide pact?

On the night of October 11, friends Neon Leon and Cathi O'Rourke, who also lived in the Chelsea Hotel, saw Nancy around midnight. At 2:30 a.m., she rang a dealer friend called Rockets Redglare and begged him to bring her some Dilaudid and needles. Rockets arrived at 3:15 a.m. having been unable to find the drug, and he found Sid and Nancy very drowsy, having taken Tuinal. Nancy showed him several wads of fifty- and hundred-dollar bills and promised to pay him over the odds if he could procure some Dilaudid. As he left the room at 5 a.m., he says he saw another dealer arrive, a man he called "Steven." At around 7:30 a.m., a hotel resident heard moaning coming from the room but did not report it. It was 10 a.m. when Sid called reception saying "Someone is sick . . . need help." When the paramedics and police arrived, they found Nancy lying dead in her underwear in the hotel bathroom with a single stab wound to her stomach. Sid was wandering around the corridors in a state of shock, crying, "I killed her. I can't live without her." Later that afternoon he was charged with her murder.

Sid was remanded to the detox unit at New York's notorious Rikers Island prison until

October 16, when the Pistols' record company posted bail. His mother Anne flew out to look after him and when he tried to commit suicide on the night of his release by cutting his wrists and overdosing on methadone, she saved his

> ## "SHE WAS THE ONLY THING THAT MATTERED TO ME.... I LIVED FOR HER. NOW I MUST DIE FOR HER"

life. He attempted suicide again and after he was admitted to Bellevue mental hospital for his own protection, he tried to jump out of the window. According to some friends he intimated that he and Nancy had made a suicide pact and he hadn't fulfilled his part in it because he'd passed out due to the effects of the Tuinal. However, he didn't have any recollection of the stabbing. By December, Sid was out of hospital and had a new girlfriend, Michele Robinson, but he was still in mourning for Nancy and wrote long letters to her mother proclaiming his feelings and telling her that he just wanted to die himself: "Nancy became my whole life," he wrote. "She was the only thing that mattered to me. . . . I lived for her. Now I must die for her."

On December 9, he was arrested after cutting the face of Todd Smith, the brother of musician Patti Smith, with a broken bottle. He was sent back to Rikers Island for seven weeks during which he endured excruciating heroin withdrawal. Upon his release on February 1, 1979, Michele threw a party in her apartment to celebrate, and Sid's mother gave him some heroin. He shot up and demanded more then collapsed on a bed. At some time during the night, he appears to have woken, injected himself with the remainder of the heroin from his mother's bag, and died. He was twenty-one years old; Nancy had been just twenty.

When Nancy's mother Deborah looked down at her daughter's body, she felt that the girl had found peace at last after all the pain of her life. Deborah refused to give permission for them to be buried together, but Anne later sprinkled Sid's ashes on Nancy's grave. There's little doubt that's what they would have wanted. No matter what they thought of her, all Sid's friends recognized how much he had been in love. "She was the first and only love of his life," said Malcolm McLaren. It was a Romeo and Juliet story for the punk generation—one with a similarly tragic ending.

"I'M GOING TO BE A SUPERSTAR MUSICIAN,
KILL MYSELF, AND GO OUT IN A FLAME OF GLORY"

KURT COBAIN
&
COURTNEY LOVE

ROCK 'N' ROLL

KURT DONALD COBAIN

Born: February 20, 1967
Aberdeen, Washington

Died: c.April 5, 1994
Seattle, Washington

COURTNEY MICHELLE HARRISON

Born: July 9, 1964
San Francisco, California

★

Married: February 24, 1992
Waikiki Beach, Hawaii

KURT COBAIN & COURTNEY LOVE

Kurt and Courtney were kindred spirits whose troubled backgrounds gave them a strong emotional connection. They loved each other with great passion and devotion, but from the start there was always a third party in the relationship—heroin.

Back in the 1960s and early '70s divorce was not common, but both Kurt and Courtney's parents divorced and they felt like outcasts in the new, extended stepfamilies that ensued. They were shunted from household to household, and by their teens they were basically homeless. It takes a lot of resilience to recover from that kind of start in life.

Courtney's mother Linda was only twenty and married to Hank Harrison, a former manager of the Grateful Dead, when she gave birth to Courtney. They divorced when she was five, and her mother was awarded custody after it transpired that Hank had fed LSD to his young daughter the previous year. Linda married a man called Frank Rodriguez who adopted Courtney, but she felt insecure when they had more children: two half-sisters and an adopted brother. She yearned for her mother's love and felt she didn't belong in this new family. Her behavior became challenging and she was diagnosed with mild autism and given a short course of Ritalin, a drug used to treat hyperactivity. She later blamed the drug for her attraction to street drugs as an adult, saying, "It was euphoric when you were a child—isn't that memory going to stick with you?" In 1972, Linda divorced Frank and moved to New Zealand. Courtney attended school there for a while, but her mother decided she couldn't cope and sent her back to live in the US with Frank Rodriguez; he also couldn't cope, so Courtney was placed in foster care in her teens.

OPPOSITE
Kurt at the Reading Festival, 1991. "There was a kind of cockiness about Nirvana that day," said a road manager. "They had a confidence."

BELOW
Courtney with Hole at Glastonbury in 1999, when the festival lineup included Blondie, Patti Smith, R.E.M., and the Manic Street Preachers.

179

ABOVE
Kurt with his parents and his sister Kim. Three years after this photo was taken his parents separated, and he wrote on his bedroom wall, "I hate Mom, I hate Dad. Dad hates Mom, Mom hates Dad. It simply makes you want to be so sad."

A social work report said of her, "Appears to be strong and capable externally, but internally a frightened young lady." At the age of sixteen, freed from state intervention in her care, she supported herself by working as a stripper and a DJ, and studied English and Philosophy at Portland State University. On one thing everyone was agreed—she was fiercely bright and articulate. While others might have been crushed by such a childhood, she emerged a tough cookie with a strong determination to succeed in life.

Kurt's mother Wendy was a very beautiful young waitress married to a car mechanic named Don. Kurt was a lively child who had an imaginary friend called Boddah, and he loved to draw cartoon characters and listen to music. When he was only seven years old, he, like Courtney, was put on a short course of Ritalin, as he was thought to have ADHD (attention deficit hyperactivity disorder). That same year, his parents separated and he reacted by feeling ashamed, as if it was his fault in some way and others would judge him for not having the perfect nuclear family. He moved in with his dad and the two were close for a while. Kurt made Don promise never to remarry—but within a couple of years he was dating a woman called Jenny, who had two kids of her own, and when they married Kurt felt left out. He couldn't go to his mother's, as she had a violent boyfriend whom Kurt once saw breaking her arm. At the age of fifteen he left home and over the next four years he would stay at ten different addresses, claiming at one point to be sleeping under a bridge. Two of his uncles had committed suicide by shooting themselves, while another drank himself to death, and Kurt told friends, "I'm going to be a superstar musician, kill myself, and go out in a flame of glory."

A hole in the soul

Courtney was a creative child with ambitions to be in a band and to act, and she was prepared to work hard to achieve her goals. In 1981 she formed a band called Sugar Babydoll with

two friends; in 1982 she wrangled her way into a band called
Faith No More; then a couple of years later she formed
Pagan Babies with Kat Bjelland, whom she met in a Portland
nightclub in 1984. She also played for a short time with Babes
in Toyland before she made the decision to start her own group
and placed an ad in a magazine. Eric Erlandson joined as lead
guitarist, Lisa Roberts was on bass guitar, Caroline Rue on
drums, and Courtney on vocals. She named the band Hole,
inspired by a quote from Euripides' *Medea* that read, "there's a
hole that pierces my soul." Their sound was influenced by punk
rock and metal and their first album, *Pretty on the Inside*, was
released in September 1991 to critical acclaim, although *Q
Magazine* described it as "loud, ugly, and deliberately shocking."

BELOW
*The Hole lineup in 1989
(from left to right): Eric
Erlandson, Courtney,
Caroline Rue, and
Kristen Pfaff. Courtney
dated Eric for a year
after the band formed.*

The single "Teenage
Whore" made number
one in Britain's indie
charts, and they began to
tour in Europe and the
US. Meanwhile, Courtney
had appeared in a small
role in the movie *Sid
and Nancy* (1986) about
punk's most infamous
couple, and in one of the
lead roles in the action
comedy *Straight to Hell*
(1986). No one could call
it an easy path to fame.
She had been paying
her dues for a decade
before she met Kurt and
became a whole lot more
famous overnight.

Kurt's uncle gave him
a guitar for his fourteenth
birthday and he taught
himself to play. He liked
punk rock and started a
punk band called Fecal
Matter in 1985, then in

A TASTE FOR DESTRUCTION

The tradition of rock stars trashing their hotel rooms has a long and venerable history. One of the first and most famous recorded instances was on the twenty-first birthday of The Who's drummer, Keith Moon, at the Holiday Inn in Flint, Michigan in 1967, when he let off fire extinguishers, threw furniture around before, as legend has it, driving a Lincoln Continental into the swimming pool. He later became notorious for destroying toilets, and always made a point of smashing up his drum kit on stage. Pete Townshend started the equipment-smashing trend, by destroying his guitar on stage in 1964, and he was followed by Jimi Hendrix, who burned his guitar at the 1967 Monterrey Festival. In 1972, Keith Richards of The Rolling Stones was filmed throwing a television off the balcony of his hotel room on LA's Sunset Strip. Led Zeppelin drummer John Bonham reportedly drove a motorcycle through the corridors of LA's Chateau Marmont and, although '80s rock stars mainly decided the habit was passé, Nirvana resurrected it, regularly destroying their instruments on stage and being banned from many hotels for trashing their rooms.

'86 he and his friend Krist Novoselic formed another band called Nirvana, named after the Buddhist state of spiritual enlightenment. They toured a lot, playing as many as a hundred gigs in 1989, but it was 1991 before they made the big breakthrough with their second album *Nevermind* and the hit single "Smells Like Teen Spirit." Both captured a style and a moment and flew straight to the top of the charts, popularizing the genre known as "grunge," a kind of loud, distorted punk. For three years while they were establishing themselves, Kurt had lived with a girl called Tracy Marander, who was by all accounts a stabilizing influence. She provided a home, complete with lots of pets: turtles, rats, cats, and a rabbit called Stew. She fed Kurt and persuaded him to give up smoking cigarettes for the sake of his voice and to cut down on his use of drugs (his drug of choice at that time was LSD).

In 1990, Tracy and Kurt broke up after the passion faded and his lifestyle became more chaotic. He was consumed with rage and self-hatred after a new girlfriend, Tobi Vail, broke up with him, and he began to write increasingly angry songs. Dinner was invariably a takeout, and it was in November that year when he overcame his childhood fear of needles and injected heroin for the first time. He'd always suffered from excruciating stomach pain, the cause of which was never definitively diagnosed, and heroin seemed to be the only thing that could ease it—or perhaps that was just a convenient excuse.

Three feathers

Courtney and Kurt first met on January 12, 1990, in a Portland nightclub called Satyricon. "You look like Dave Pirner," she said, referring to the floppy-haired singer in the band Soul

"I'VE MET THE COOLEST GIRL IN THE WHOLE WORLD"

Asylum. Kurt reacted unexpectedly by wrestling her to the floor, which was sticky with spilled beer, then gave her a monkey sticker by way of apology. "She looked like a classic punk rock chick," he said later. "I did feel kind of attracted to her." Courtney was glad to have got his attention, but surprised to discover that he was shorter than her and began referring to him to friends as "Pixie Meat." They met again in May 1991, at the Palladium in LA, and this time she gave him her phone number. He called at 3 a.m. that morning and they talked for over an hour, after which he told a friend, "I've met the coolest girl in the whole world." She was in a relationship with Billy Corgan of The Smashing Pumpkins but she knew she liked Kurt. Five months later, she went to a Nirvana gig in Europe, broke up with Billy, and finally she and Kurt ended up in bed together. He told friends that the sex was amazing but, more than that, they had a huge shared emotional connection—they both knew what it was like to be shuttled between divorced parents, unhappy at school, poor, and homeless. At last each had met another human being who seemed to understand exactly what it was like to be them.

BELOW
Dave Grohl, Kurt, and Krist Novoselic on tour in Germany, November 1991, just after Kurt and Courtney got together. "At times I even forget I'm in a band, I'm so blinded by love," he told a journalist.

ABOVE
Kurt's mom said, "they were like clones, glued to each other . . . He was probably the only person who loved her totally and completely unconditionally."

On their second date, back in the US, Kurt suggested they take heroin, and Courtney hesitated, because she hated needles, but then agreed. While high, they went for a walk together and came across a dead bird lying on the ground. Kurt pulled off three feathers and gave one to Courtney, saying that one was for her, one for him, and one for the baby they would have together. She later said that was the moment when she began to fall in love with him. The next day he wanted to do more heroin but Courtney refused. "I had a rule about not doing drugs two nights in a row." But without shooting up, Kurt was in terrible pain from his stomach so to keep him company she eventually decided to break her self-imposed rule. Friends and fellow band members were alarmed when they realized that Courtney was taking drugs with him and that his consumption was increasing, but no one could say anything because the couple were so besotted with each other. When they went on tour with their respective bands, they spoke on the phone every night and sent faxes to each other. "You smell like waffles and milk . . . I love and miss your body and your twenty-minute kisses," she wrote. Kurt grabbed a microphone and announced live on British television, "I just want everyone to know that Courtney Love, of the pop group Hole, is the best fuck in the world."

In December 1991, they got engaged while lying in bed in a London hotel room, and shortly afterward Courtney discovered she was pregnant. At first they were both terrified that the heroin she had taken before she realized she was pregnant might have harmed the child. She detoxed immediately and Kurt tried to stop as well but couldn't stick to it. Courtney encouraged him by breaking any syringes she found around the house and refusing to put through any phone calls from dealers, but his consumption increased until he was getting through $400-worth a day. They married in February 1992, on Waikiki Beach in Hawaii, Courtney wearing a vintage silk dress while Kurt wore green plaid pajamas, and on August 18, the daughter they called Frances Bean was born. Kurt fainted in the delivery room, and was thrilled and scared at the same time by this new little person they had created. Courtney was delighted to be a mom and wrote, "We knew we could give [Frances] what we didn't get: loyalty and compassion, encouragement." But all their plans were thrown up in the air when social workers arrived, having been alerted to the couple's drug use by an article in *Vanity Fair*. There followed a series of court hearings in which it was decided that the baby should not be left with Kurt or Courtney but should be cared for by court-approved guardians with the parents being granted supervised access. All of a sudden, Courtney was branded a bad mother by the media; she was both furious and desperately upset.

BELOW
While she was in the womb, Kurt and Courtney called their baby "Little Bean," so after she was born she became Frances Bean Cobain.

A death wish

Kurt and Courtney continued to be inseparable, writing in the same journal, composing songs together, and reading to each other in bed. She was delighted when Frances was legally returned to their care when she was seven months old, and they both loved being parents. "My daughter Frances, a cherubic joy,

THE 27 CLUB

"Now he's gone and joined that stupid club," Kurt's mom said after his death, appearing to refer to the 27 Club, an unofficial grouping of rock musicians who all died at the age of twenty-seven. There was a slew of them between 1969 and 1971—Brian Jones of The Rolling Stones, who succumbed to a mixture of alcohol, drugs, and a swimming pool; Jimi Hendrix, who combined strong sleeping pills with alcohol; Janis Joplin and Jim Morrison of The Doors, who both seem to have overdosed on heroin. These all appeared to be accidental deaths, but Kurt's was a very deliberate suicide, as was that of Pete Ham of Badfinger, who hanged himself in his garage. Two months after Kurt's death, Kristen Pfaff of Courtney's band Hole died of a heroin overdose in the bath at her Seattle apartment. And seventeen years later, Amy Winehouse died in her bed in London of accidental alcohol poisoning, having always expressed a fear of dying at that age. Some rock fans have suggested that there seems to be a statistical spike in the number of musicians dying at twenty-seven and that Kurt might have deliberately chosen to join them.

taught me to be more tolerant of all humanity," Kurt wrote. The problem was that he needed parenting, too, and Courtney couldn't take care of all three of them. They began to have wild fights and the police were called on several occasions. Kurt was using a very high level of heroin and during 1993 he accidentally overdosed a number of times. It was terrifying for Courtney, but she and Frances's nanny developed a sequence of strategies to revive him. They threw cold water on his face, walked him around, and injected him with Narcan, a drug used to counteract heroin overdoses, of which Courtney had laid in a supply—then if all else had failed they called the paramedics. In March 1994, while Kurt was on a European tour with Nirvana, Courtney flew out to Rome to see him. That night, as she lay beside him, he made his first serious suicide attempt, writing a note in which he accused his wife of sleeping with her ex-boyfriend Billy Corgan, then swallowing sixty Rohypnol tablets, a strong sedative. Courtney woke and got him to hospital, where he spent twenty hours in a coma before coming round.

Back home in Seattle, a group consisting of friends, family, and band managers staged an intervention, confronting Kurt about his heroin use and one by one telling him he had to stop. Courtney said, "You have to be a good daddy," and told him that if he didn't get himself off drugs she would divorce him and he would only have limited access to Frances. She had slipped off the wagon herself and was about to begin rehab in a hotel in Los Angeles. Kurt was furious and Courtney left the next morning without getting so much as a goodbye kiss from her husband. Then on March 30, 1994, he arrived at LA's Exodus Recovery Center to begin his own treatment before two days later he climbed a fence and disappeared. Courtney was frantic, calling every drug dealer she could think of to try and track him down. After a couple of days when there was no sign of him, she hired private investigators, though still with no success. Then at 8.40 a.m. on April 8, an electrician arrived at their home on Lake Washington Boulevard, Seattle, and saw a body in the greenhouse. Kurt had written a long, rambling suicide note addressed to his imaginary childhood friend Boddah, injected one last fix of heroin, then shot himself through the head with a shotgun.

KURT COBAIN
(1967 — 1994)

Courtney rushed to the scene and insisted on putting on her husband's blood-speckled corduroy coat. In the days after his death she liked to wear his clothes because she could still smell him on them. In the funeral home she climbed on top of his body, crying, "Why, why why?" And at a memorial service on April 10, she bravely read out his suicide note to the 7,000 mourners, interspersed with her own furious commentary. When the note read, "It's better to burn out than fade away," she cried, "Don't remember this because it is a fucking lie."

> ## "IF HE CAME BACK RIGHT NOW, I'D HAVE TO KILL HIM FOR WHAT HE DID TO US"

Kurt and Courtney were similar souls drawn to each other for that reason, but she was stronger, she was a survivor, and has gone on to make many successful albums and movies since his death. She dated actor Edward Norton for three years and was also linked to comedian Steve Coogan, but has never remarried. It's hard to recover from the suicide of someone you have loved so deeply, and even in recent years Courtney has expressed her furious anger with Kurt. "If he came back right now, I'd have to kill him for what he did to us," she says. "I'd fuck him, and then I'd kill him."

ABOVE
Kurt's death is announced in NME, April 16, 1994. At the end of his suicide note, he wrote, "Please keep going Courtney, for Frances. For her life, which will be so much happier without me. I LOVE YOU, I LOVE YOU!"

INDEX

INDEX

Johnny Cash & June Carter

Cash, John Carter. *Anchored in Love*. New York, Thomas Nelson: 2007.
Miller, Stephen. *Johnny Cash: The Life of an American Icon*. New York, Omnibus Press: 2003.
Turner, Stephen. *The Man Called CASH: The Life, Love, and Faith of an American Legend*. Nashville, W Publishing: 2004.

Ike & Tina Turner

Turner, Ike. *Taking Back My Name: The Confessions of Ike Turner*. London, Virgin Publishing: 1999.
Turner, Tina, with Loder, Kurt. *I, Tina*. New York, William Morrow & Co: 1986.
Winfrey, Oprah, interview with Tina Turner in *O, The Oprah Magazine*, October 2005.

Elvis Presley & Priscilla Beaulieu

Goldman, Albert. *Elvis*. New York, McGraw–Hill: 1981.
Guralnick, Peter. *Last Train to Memphis*. New York, Little Brown: 1994.
Presley, Priscilla Beaulieu, with Sandra Harmon. *Elvis and Me*. Putnam, New York, Century Hutchison: 1985.

Bob Dylan & Joan Baez

Dylan, Bob. *Chronicles, Volume 1*. New York, Simon & Schuster: 2005.
Hajdu, David, *Positively 4th Street*. New York, Farrar, Straus and Giroux: 2001.
Shelton, Robert. *No Direction Home*. Cambridge, Mass., Da Capo Press: 2003.

Sonny & Cher

Bono, Sonny. *And the Beat Goes On*. New York, Simon & Schuster: 1991.
Cher, with Jeff Coplon. *The First Time*. New York, Simon & Schuster: 1998.
Taraborelli, Randy. *Cher*. New York, St. Martin's Press: 1986.

George Harrison & Pattie Boyd

Boyd, Pattie, with Penny Junor. *Wonderful Today*. London, Headline: 2007.
Harrison, George. *I Me Mine*. London, Chronicle Books: 2007.
Tillery, Gary. *Working Class Mystic*. Wheaton, IL, Quest Books: 2011.

Mick Jagger & Marianne Faithfull

Faithfull, Marianne, with Dalton, David. *Faithfull*. London, Michael Joseph: 1994.
Norman, Philip. *Mick Jagger*. London, HarperCollins: 2012.

John Lennon & Yoko Ono

Clayson, Alan. *Woman: The Incredible Life of Yoko Ono*. London, Chrome Dreams: 2004.
Norman, Philip. *John Lennon*. London, HarperCollins: 2008.

Ono, Yoko. *Grapefruit: A Book of Instructions and Drawings*. New York, Simon & Schuster: 2000.

Serge Gainsbourg & Jane Birkin

Brophy, Gwenda. "Time and Place: Jane Birkin." London, *The Sunday Times*: 2009.

Robinson, Lisa. "The Secret World of Serge Gainsbourg." New York, *Vanity Fair*: 2007.

Simmons, Sylvie. *Serge Gainsbourg: A Fistful of Gitanes*. Cambridge, Mass., Da Capo Press: 2002.

James Taylor & Carly Simon

Farndale, Nigel. "Carly Simon interview." London, *Telegraph*: 2010.

Halperin, Ian. *Fire and Rain: The James Taylor Story*. New York, Citadel Press: 2000.

Weller, Sheila. *Girls Like Us: Carole King, Joni Mitchell, Carly Simon—and the Journey of a Generation*. New York, Washington Square Press: 2009.

Lou Reed & Laurie Anderson

Bockris, Victor. *Lou Reed: The Biography*. New York, Hutchison: 1994.

Laurie Anderson's biography from her website at www.laurieanderson.com

Lou Reed's last interview for *Rolling Stone*, pub. November 21, 2013: www.rollingstone.com/music/videos/lou–reeds–last–words–watch–his–final–interview–20131108

Debbie Harry & Chris Stein

Che, Cathay. *Deborah Harry: Platinum Blonde*. London, Andre Deutsch: 1999.

Harry, Debbie, Stein, Chris, and Bockris, Victor. *Making Tracks: The Rise of Blondie*. Cambridge, Mass., Da Capo Press: 1998.

Porter, Dick, and Needs, Chris. *Blondie, Parallel Lives*. London, Omnibus Press: 2012.

Sid Vicious & Nancy Spungen

Parker, Alan. *Vicious: Too Fast to Live*. London, Creation Books: 2004.

Parker, Alan. *No One is Innocent*, London, Orion: 2008.

Spungen, Deborah. *And I Don't Want to Live This Life*. New York, Ballantine Books: 2011.

Kurt Cobain & Courtney Love

Cross, Charles. *Heavier than Heaven: The Biography of Kurt Cobain*. New York, Hyperion: 2001.

Love, Courtney. *Dirty Blonde: The Diaries of Courtney Love*. New York, Faber & Faber: 2006.

O'Brien, Lucy. *She Bop: The Definitive History of Women in Rock, Pop and Soul*. New York, Continuum: 1995.

Corbis/Denis O'Regan: 173; Lawrence Schwartzwald/Sygma: 149

Getty Images/Richard E. Aaron/Redferns: 130; Roberta Bayley/ Redferns: 152, 154, 158; Paul Bergen/Redferns: 183; Blank Archives: 61; Botti/Gamma-Keystone: 124; Columbia Records: 58; Evening Standard: 95; Fox Photos: 13; GAB Archive/Redferns: 26, 157; Ron Galella: 137; Gems/Redferns: 143; Gijsbert Hanekroot/Redferns: 103; Hulton Archive: 94; Yale Joel/Time & Life Pictures: 23; Keystone-France/Gamma-Keystone: 82, 121; George Lipman/The Sydney Morning Herald/Fairfax Media: 92; Terry McGinnis/WireImage: 184; Joe McNally: 139; Leon Morris/Redferns: 146; Paul Natkin: 145; Martin O'Neill/Redferns: 17; Michael Ochs Archives: 6, 7, 9, 10, 11, 24, 32, 36, 50, 99, 107, 128, 133, 147, 156, 160; RDA: 122; Jack Robinson/Hulton Archive: 134; Lex van Rossen/MAI/Redferns: 162; Eric Schaal/Time & Life Pictures: 25; Daniel Simon/Gamma-Rapho: 127; Bill Stahl Jr./NY Daily News Archive: 19T; Virginia Turbett/ Redferns: 171; James Whitmore/Time & Life Pictures: 48

ImageCollect.com/Globe Photos: 8, 12, 16, 19B, 20, 22, 27, 29, 30, 31, 34, 39T, 40, 41, 42, 43, 44, 46, 47, 49, 51, 52, 54, 55, 56, 59, 60, 64, 65, 66, 67, 68, 70, 73, 74, 75, 76, 77, 78, 79, 80, 83, 84, 85, 86, 87, 89, 90, 91, 96, 98, 101T, 101B, 102, 104, 106, 108, 109, 110, 111, 112, 113, 114, 115, 116, 118, 119, 123, 125, 136, 142, 144, 151, 159, 163, 174, 176, 179; StarMaxWorldwide: 140; Zumapress: 14, 39B, 150

Library of Congress, Washington, D.C.: 63

National Archives and Records Administration: 62

Photoshot/A. Indge/Retna: 181; LFI: 166; Retna: 170; Paul Slattery/Retna: 164

Rex: 180, 187; David Dagley: 169; Everett Collection: 71; Ray Stevenson: 172; Geoffrey Swaine: 178; Stephen Sweet: 185; Warner Brothers/Everett: 138